The Beginning
of
Her Story

by

Crystal Ann Mitchell

DORRANCE
PUBLISHING CO
EST. 1920
PITTSBURGH, PENNSYLVANIA 15238

Dorrance Publishing Co
585 Alpha Drive
Pittsburgh, PA 15238
Visit our website at *www.dorrancebookstore.com*

ISBN: 978-1-4809-9170-5
eISBN: 978-1-4809-8993-1

For my brother,

LaRoz Lee Mitchell

Chapter One

"I usually find myself dazing back into the past... I sometimes wish I could start over from a specific date and time."

Tears fell down my cheeks, and I covered my face with my hands so he couldn't see. I could feel my face was hot. I was shaking, and I bust out crying. The room was scary silent, so all I could hear was my cry. Minutes had passed when I felt a headache coming on. I wiped my eyes with the back of my hands only to find him with his legs crossed, staring straight into my soul.

"Ms. Guy, do you think you can continue, or would you like to stop here and next week continue or-"

"No, I'm fine. I'm fine," I replied, cutting him off.

He moved his hand out, motioning me to continue on. I glanced at the clock and realized we were only 15 minutes into my first session. My body temperature had returned back to normal, and I was no longer shaking. I leaned my head back on the cozy brown loveseat and closed my eyes. I inhaled and then exhaled, thinking to myself, *Meagan, people have betrayed you, but he's not them. Go ahead and tell him. You would probably feel a whole lot better.*

I opened my eyes, raised my head up, and took another glance at him. He nodded to confirm he was ready whenever I was. I inhaled and exhaled again, thinking to myself, *Here it goes.*

Chapter Two

"About six years ago… I was working at this nursing home as a nurse aide. I have been a nurse aide for about six years by this time, and that's when I met him… He didn't look friendly at all, and to be honest, not even my type." I giggled and glanced at my psychologist, and he nodded for me to continue with a straight face.

"I was being trained by a girl, and he was working on the same hall as us. And I can't really remember if my trainer left to go on a doctor's appointment or if she was pulled because this nursing home was always shorthanded - but whatever it was caused me to take the group by myself. It was like my second day there, and basically I was thrown to the wolves. And that's when he had to come to me and walk me through each resident that I was going to have."

"You never told me his name, Ms. Guy," Dr. Martin said. My throat was dry, so I reached for my bottled water that was on the glass table in front of me.

Dr. Martin looked at me, waiting for my response. I took a deep breath and lowered my head down and answered, "David," in a low voice.

"Okay, continue," Dr. Martin said while reaching for a pen and a notepad on the small glass table beside his brown chair.

"Well…" I paused. "…David showed me the group and actually explained in great detail about each resident I was to be taking care of. He was actually friendly, and my first impression of him was wrong." I leaned my head back on the brown loveseat and stared at the ceiling, as if a film projector was replaying my life, and I was watching so I could retell it.

"He actually was sooo kind that we had become good friends."

"Good friends like how, Ms. Guy?" Dr. Martin asked with a smile on his face. This was the first time this man had smiled since I had been here.

"Well, we would go out to eat on Fridays. He was much older than me, so the things he would do would make me feel special. It's kind of hard to explain, but I was in a relationship with a guy at this time. My mate and I were together for about eight years, and he never wanted to do anything special or go out. So, when I met David, he did things that I wish my lover would have done," I explained.

Dr. Martin seemed to be getting interested in my story now. He uncrossed his legs, folded his arms, and with a smile to melt your heart. "Continue."

"David became my best friend, and I'm not going to lie we, we..."

Dr. Martin was shaking his head as to assure me it's okay to tell him what he already knew what I was going to say. I glanced at the clock on the wall and noticed my time was up.

"Um, Dr. Martin, look at the time," I said.

He looked at the time and was shocked by how time snuck by.

"Oh okay, Ms. Guy. So when will our next session be next week?"

"How about we make it the same day and same time?" I replied.

He went to his computer desk in the corner of the room.

"Next Tuesday at 4 o'clock sounds okay with me."

I grabbed my brown Coach purse along with my bottled water, and headed for the door. As I turned the doorknob, Dr. Martin called my name, and I turned.

"You had sex with him?"

I looked at him.

"You had sex with David while in a relationship with another man?" he asked.

"Yes, I did, Dr. Martin," I said, and quickly exited out of his office, wondering why I was even talking to him about my problems anyways.

Chapter Three

I was 10 minutes early pulling up to Dr. Martin's private office. I had pulled my eyeliner out of my purse, adjusted and looked through the rearview mirror, and put my eyeliner on. I then pulled my brown lipstick out. *Naw,* I thought to myself and threw the lipstick back into my purse.

"Meagan, what are you doing? Why are you even here?" I asked myself aloud.

A black four-door Mercedes had parked on the left side of me. The windows were tinted, so when the driver side door opened, I realized it was Dr. Martin. His suit and suitcase matched his car. He was 5' 9" with slim build and caramel complexion, weighing about 144 pounds, rocking a bald head with a beard. I never cared for guys with bald heads, but he was what you call eye candy.

I was watching him while he was talking on his iPhone, wondering who he was talking to, specifically if he had a special lady at home, or if he was a dog like most men.

I must have been really mesmerized because when he pressed his alarm for his car to lock, I jumped, only to see him motioning me to come.

"Here's day two of telling my business," I whispered to myself, as I opened my door to step out of the car.

Chapter Four

As Dr. Martin unlocked the door to his office, I was standing behind him shivering. It was 40 degrees, and the Lord knows I hate the cold.

"So, how are you liking this November weather?" he asked, as he swung open the door.

"I don't," I replied while entering his office.

"I myself don't care for this weather. I would rather be in Florida on a beach enjoying 80- degree weather," he said, chuckling.

"Me too," I said, looking around in the dark room.

He went towards the restroom and turned on the lights. The room was warm and cozy, which I was glad.

"I had left the heat running because I knew I was going to be just right on time today. I have psychic powers. I just knew you hated the cold," he joked, and we both laughed.

"Please sit."

I plopped down on the loveseat, as he hung his black dress coat up on the coat rack and walked over to his chair. He reached for his pen and notepad on the glass table beside him. Dr. Martin then licked his finger and turned a few pages. He then looked at me with a serious look on his face, said, "Well, we're at the part when you and David became friends."

My hands felt sweaty and hot, and my throat felt dry. Reminiscing back to the best days between David and I was nice. How can a person make you feel so special, but yet you're in a relationship with someone else?

"Ms. Guy, are you okay?" Dr. Martin asked while jotting down notes in his notepad.

I looked up at the ceiling. "Yes. I mean, he had no kids. He had two jobs - plus, he was a student at a university. He had his own house and car and single."

My boyfriend at the time, his name was Jason. Jason lived with me and my daughter whom he helped me raise because her father… Well, let's just say Jason took the role her biological father didn't want to play.

"I had been having a crush on Jason ever since I was 13. He was a little older than me. To tell the truth, I don't think Jason looked twice at me in that kind of way back then," I said, smirking.

Jason was 6' 1", slim, dark-skinned, and he stole my heart for years. It wasn't until I was 19 years old with a three-month-old daughter, living in the projects, when my best friend, Renee, hooked us up.

"Jason had no kids when we hooked up, and he had no job, but had wads of money whenever he came to my house."

Dr. Martin glanced up from his notepad. "How did he have wads of money with no job?"

In my mind I was thinking, *You know.*

"He sold drugs. I was on welfare, which paid for my nurse aide classes, and that's how I became a nurse aide. Jason actually helped buy things for my apartment, and he also got us clothes and shoes. Jason took on the role of being a father to my daughter, and to this day, she loves him dearly."

"What's your daughter's name, if you don't mind me asking?" Dr. Martin asked.

"Haylen," I replied.

It wasn't always peaches and cream between Jason and I. We've had our ups and downs. And after two years of us being together, we decided to move in together, so we moved into an apartment across town.

"Did you and Jason have any children together?" Dr. Martin asked.

"Yes. September 12, 2008, we had a son. His name was Mekhi Lee Carpenter."

"You said 'was' in the past tense, so you're saying he's no longer living?"

"Correct. Mekhi and my granny, Virginia Bell, died on the same day. He was a stillborn." I looked down at my brown Coach fur boots.

"Wow. I'm so sorry to hear that, Ms. Guy. How did you handle those two losses at once?"

"Well, I smoked some weed from time to time, and then I bought a Shih Tzu puppy from my hall nurse, and that was comforting to my daughter and me."

Chapter Five

The room fell silent, and it felt good to talk about my pain that I had kept inside all these years. I mean, losing a child and your granny who helped raise you was hard to accept.

"So how do you feel about your deceased grandmother and son now, if you don't mind me asking?" Dr. Martin asked.

"I sometimes block it out and act as if they're just away in another state. I actually do that with all deaths. I think that's how I cope with all deaths."

"I see. So, after the death of your son, how was your and Jason's relationship?" Dr. Martin asked.

"It was okay, I guess. I worked first shift, and he got a job working third shift. He really never liked doing anything to make me feel special, unless I bitched at him, and then he would *try*. It was like we were scared to move on and find better."

"So, when you met David, he'd done things you wished Jason would have done, so when did you come to terms of ending your relationship?" Dr. Martin asked while picking his notepad from his lap.

"Well, Jason and I would fight mostly over dumb shit, and my daughter would be present most of those times. One morning, I was getting ready for work, and Jason was supposed to drop Haylen off at school so I wouldn't be late for work. We had to go to the gas station. For some reason, we got into a fight in front of my daughter. I had to go to work late because he refused to take her to school. I saw David that morning at work and told him I was done with Jason, and of course, he was happy."

"So, did you and David get together right after you and Jason ended your relationship?"

"No, it wasn't until a year later that David and I would get together."

I looked at the clock on the wall and saw out of my peripheral that Dr. Martin's eyes had followed.

"Well, it's that time, huh?" Dr. Martin asked while getting up from his chair to walk over to his desktop computer to schedule me for our next session.

"Yeeesssss," I sighed. Deep down inside, I can't wait to see this man. Oh, how the week goes by so slowly, and the actual day I see him time flies by.

"Same time?" he asked, as he turned to look at me.

With a smile, I answered, "Yes."

I got up from the loveseat and walked towards the door. Then Dr. Martin said, "Well, my client had emailed me rescheduling their session. So, since I have nothing planned, would you like to go for coffee or a bite to eat?"

My soul glowed, and my caramel complexion probably allowed my cheeks to turn rosey red.

"I would love to but…" His smile disappeared. *Oh, how white and pretty his teeth are*, I thought. "…I have to get home and cook dinner."

"I understand. Maybe there will be another day."

Deep down inside, I was wishing the time would be now.

"Yeah, maybe another day." I turned the knob and opened the door, and the cold air smacked me in my face. It was starting to snow.

I looked back at Dr. Martin, who was now putting his dress coat on.

"Have yourself a good evening, Dr. Martin. See you next week," I said.

"That's if we don't get snowed in," Dr. Martin replied. "You know this Kentucky weather is something else. We don't know what to expect."

We both laughed, as we exited the door.

"Be careful," we both said at the same time, then laughed again.

We both got in our cars, and I heard my phone ring.

"Hello," I answered.

"So, how did it go?" David asked.

"I'm on my way home. We can talk there," I responded, then hung up the phone with disgust.

Chapter Six

I was running late to see Dr. Martin, so when I reached his office, it was 4:15 P.M.. He was sitting in his chair with his black iPhone in his hand. "I was getting worried about you," Dr. Martin said. He put his phone aside on the table next to him and grabbed his pen and notepad.

"I'm sorry," I replied, finding my way to the loveseat.

"Well, the good thing is that you've made it safely. That snow out there can make it dangerous for anyone to drive in," he said while repositioning himself in his chair.

"So, what part of Florida are you from?" I asked while rubbing my hands together.

"Lauderdale Lakes," Dr. Martin answered. "I'm assuming that you've been here in Kentucky all your life?" he asked, staring at me with those big, brown, innocent, bedroom eyes.

"Unfortunately, yes," I sighed with a forced, fake smile on my face.

While turning pages in his notepad, he said, "Well, it's never too late to travel." After about a half-minute pause, he continued by saying, "I believe we're at the part where you and David started seeing each other after you and Jason's breakup."

"Oh, yes. David and I." I looked out the window to see the beautiful white snowflakes twirling down from the gloomy grey sky.

Not moving my eyes from the window, my mind went back into time, reliving the best part of my life with David.

"Meagan, I tell you all the time since the first day I saw you I loved you," David said.

"How can you love a person that you don't even know, David?" I asked.

David was 5' 6" - short to me, since I usually dated tall guys - so he was actually something new.

"I told you - you were my mother, my lover, my-"

"Stop, David!" I interrupted him. "Plus, I told you that I don't like mixing business with pleasure," I added.

"Give me a chance, Meagan. Just give me a chance, please."

David and I would normally work on separate units unless I volunteered to go to his unit when they were short-staffed. I would find myself volunteering all the time to work on David's unit. And the nights that I would have sex with him, having to see him at work in the mornings would send me into "straight attitude" mode, and I don't know why.

"You're fucking him, bitch," my friend Vince whispered, while smiling in my face. "You and David are fucking!" he repeated.

"Noooooooooooo," I replied while trying to keep the embarrassing truthful smile from showing.

Vince was my friend, as well as a friend of David, but I've known Vince longer.

"Well, you should mess with him," Vince insisted.

I ignored his comment while walking to get some clean linen to put on one of my resident's bed. David and I kept it a secret, but some of our coworkers had a feeling we were messing around. Outside of work, we could be ourselves, and he met my family and spent time with my daughter and I. He was welcomed to my house a lot, and we lived just a few blocks away from each other.

"Meagan, let's be together," David said.

"Well, David, I'm not ready. I've been in a relationship for years, and I'm not ready."

Chapter Seven

"So, Ms. Guy, David insisted that you two be together, but it was you that kept putting it off?" Dr. Martin asked, drawing my attention from the window.

"Yes," I replied. "We were still working together," I added.

"Ok, so when did you start dating David?" Dr. Martin asked.

"Well, after I ended up leaving that nursing home to go work at another nursing home, closer to my house," I replied.

"You said some people at the nursing home assumed that you and David were fooling around like Vince. Were there others?" Dr. Martin asked.

"Well, there were women working there that liked him, but they were no threat to me. Two women started working there, and I met them at the time clock. One of them I had known for quite some time because we had worked together before. Her name was Mary. The other woman I knew of because both of our families are really close, somewhat like family. Her name was Sherry. She and I would become very close due to our families' history, and we could talk about anything to one another. She would tell me things about her love life, and I would tell her about my love life when I was with Jason."

"So did she know about you and David?" Dr. Martin asked.

"I'm pretty sure she did. She came to me and told me how Mary liked David and how Mary thought David and I were together. I responded back telling her that David wanted to but I didn't want to mix business with pleasure. And she told me I shouldn't care what anyone thinks about me and him and how I should talk to him. And I told her he was a trick."

"Now when you say trick do you mean-"

"He would spend his money on me," I interrupted him.

"Aw, I see and by him spending money on you, what would he do?" Dr. Martin asked.

"Shower me and my daughter with gifts. He even insisted for me to be added onto his phone plan with AT&T. He even invited my daughter and me to his professor's house for a pool party on Memorial Day. And on the 4th of July, I invited him to my house to spend time with my mother, sister, cousin, and of course, my daughter, Haylen. We barbequed and watched the fireworks. We had a good time and my family really thought I should give David a chance."

"It wasn't until my friend Sherry became pregnant with twins. She told me how she wanted to abort the twins because she was considered high risk and had problems with her previous pregnancy. I pleaded to her to not have an abortion and shortly after that she left the nursing home. I left the nursing home after she left and started working at another nursing home, which was the nursing home closer to my home. That's when David and I became more intimate."

I looked at the clock, and my phone rung. It was David calling.

"Well, I guess next week, same time," I said to Dr. Martin, as he was jotting notes. He got up and walked to his desktop computer.

Just watching him made me wish I had a man like him in my life.

"Okay, see you next week," Dr. Martin replied.

"Hello," I answered my phone, as I was exiting out the door.

"What's up? Are you done?" David asked.

Instantly, I caught an attitude. "Yes, I'm on my way home now!" then I hung up.

Chapter Eight

I was sitting on the loveseat, waiting for Dr. Martin to get off the phone, when I noticed two beautiful framed pictures on the wall. One picture was of the San Francisco skyline, on the left of me, and the other framed picture was of a Vermont maple tree forest, on the right of me. Turning my attention back to Dr. Martin, he was now looking concerned, as he glanced at me from his desktop while trying to whisper. He ended his call by saying, "I love you."

Aw shit, he's taken, and she's a lucky gal, I thought to myself.

Dr. Martin walked to his chair. "So, how are you, Ms. Guy?" he asked with a smile, while reaching for his pen and notepad.

Behind him was a four-level bookshelf filled with psychology books, and plants lined the top of the bookshelf. On the wall above the bookshelf were framed degrees and his psychologist license.

"I'm here. How about yourself?"

"Aw, I'm grateful. That was my mother on the phone telling me that my sister beat her breast cancer," Dr. Martin replied.

"Well, that's great news!" I responded, happily. "Are they here in Kentucky or in Florida?"

"Back home in Florida. I'll be going home to visit soon." He flipped through his notepad.

"So, you and David became more intimate after you left the nursing home you two were both working at, and you started working at another nursing home, right?" Dr. Martin asked, glancing up from the notepad.

"Correct," I replied. I crossed my right leg over my left leg.

"I was starting to have feelings for him, and actually, I could see myself being in a relationship with him." I paused and was staring, witnessing the past, relooking at David and myself.

"Let's go shopping the day after Christmas, so I can get the sales, David," I said to him.

"Okay. That'll be fine," he replied.

I worked 7 P.M. till 7 A.M. Friday through Sunday, and Christmas landed on a Sunday that year. So when I would get off Monday morning, all I would have to do was get in the shower and put some clothes on, and we could head out.

When I got off on Christmas morning, I stayed up and watched Haylen open her Christmas presents. Watching her play with her toys made me happy to witness her as the happiest child on Earth. Having to be at work at 7 P.M., I laid down, and my phone started to ring. It was my friend Suzanne. She had followed me to the new nursing home, and we worked the same shift. I figured, whatever, she had to tell me could wait until we got to work. She called back, I ignored the call, and then she called back again. This time I had turned my phone off, so I could finally get some sleep.

I awakened around 6 P.M., and that's when my sister, Alice, had come up the stairs and said, "Tina said Sherry has died!"

"Who's Tina?" Dr. Martin asked.

"Aw, Tina is our mother. Alice just calls her Tina, and I call her Mama." Dr. Martin nodded for me to continue.

I cried, I was saddened, and I was shocked to know that someone I had become close with had actually died. It messed me up, so I called into work and told them I would be 30 minutes late because I was trying to get myself together.

I called David, and he answered the phone, and I asked him if he heard the news about Sherry. Then busted out crying again.

In a low voice, he answered, "Yeah, I tried calling you, but your phone was going straight to voicemail."

We both talked about how when I get off work the next morning we would still go shopping and then have breakfast. Then we both hung up.

I then had to get ready for work; oh how it was going to be a long 12 hours with the loss of my friend on my mind.

Chapter Nine

I got to work around 7:30 P.M., and it was the talk all over the nursing home how Sherry had died. Many people were saddened as well because she had worked there right before she came to work with David and I.

I made it through my 12-hour shift, so when I got home I took a shower, put on some clothes, and waited for David to pull up at my house. My daughter was still asleep, and my sister was living with us, so she was going to keep Haylen for me, since she helped me out a lot with her.

David pulled up in front of my house and was making his way to my front porch, and that's when I greeted him at the door.

"You ready, Meagan?" he asked while staring me up and down.

"Yeah," I replied while smiling.

I locked my door, and we both entered his four-door Nissan Merina and headed to the shopping center in Hamburg Pavilion.

We were talking, and he was asking about us taking our friendship to another level. I recall telling him that he was a nice guy and that I would probably break his heart.

"Why did you feel that you would break his heart?" Dr. Martin asked.

I paused and looked up to the ceiling.

"I think it's because I don't think I've ever been truly loved by any man that I've been involved with. I mean, I believe they loved me, but not truly faithful to me. And if you're not going to be faithful to me, then I'm not going to be faithful to you. So with David being so kind, I was feeling that maybe I wouldn't know how to treat him."

"Oh, I see," Dr. Martin replied.

As we turned into the Hamburg Pavilion shopping center, David said, "I have something to tell you."

"What?" I replied, smiling.

"I want to wait until after we shop, and I'll tell you when we eat."

I think his facial expression made me think it was something serious because I remember demanding, "Nooooo, tell me now!"

He was silent and looked scared. I then started asking, "Did you burn me? What is it?"

He pulled the car over in a parking space and turned his car off. My heart was beating fast, and I just know he's going to tell me he has given me a sexually transmitted disease.

"Tell me now, David!" I yelled.

He turned to me with these sad eyes, and his lips were moving, and I thought I heard wrong so I asked, "What did you just say?" and he repeated, "Sherry's twins are my twins, and they're still at the hospital. Do you want to go see them?"

My heart dropped into my stomach. I felt sick literally to my stomach.

"Take me home!" I demanded.

David started his car up without saying a word, and the whole ride home I kept gagging while saying, "I'm sick to my stomach!"

He never said a word. He was quiet the whole ride back to my house.

That feeling I felt that day I never want to feel again. It was like my soul walked out of my body.

He pulled up to my house, and I told him I never wanted to see him again before slamming his car door. I entered into my house, and all I could think about was how I was betrayed by two people I thought were my friends.

Chapter Ten

Dr. Martin's facial expression let me know that he was in shock. Shit. I was too reliving that sick disgusting moment, and it was like another blow to my heart.

"So, Ms. Guy," Dr. Martin said while clearing his throat. "How did you handle this betrayal?"

"Well, it's been about six years, and I still think about it from time to time. Not like I used to, but I think as time went by I started to accept that it is what it is," I answered.

"Ms. Guy, so you're telling me that you just put it in the back of your mind and forgave David?" Dr. Martin asked, as he leaned forward from his brown chair, looking straight into my eyes.

"Well, of course not. I was angry and had my mind set that I wasn't going to go to Sherry's funeral. A couple of days had passed, and I got a phone call from David just hours before Sherry's funeral. I didn't know why he was calling, so I answered the phone."

"What, David?" I answered.

"Meagan, please can I come over and talk to you?" David asked in a soft, sad voice.

"Talk about what, David?" I snapped.

"Well, my brother is here in town, so can I please come over and take a shower and so we can talk?" he begged. "Please, Meagan, please?"

"Okay," I said, and not long after we hung up, he was knocking at my door.

I let him in and walked up the stairs to my bedroom, and he followed. Just before I reached my bedroom door, he stopped me and fell to his knees, hugging my waist.

"Get off of me, David!" I demanded.

"Meagan, I'm sorry! It was a one-night stand. And I know I messed up, but I love you and want to be with you. I was scared to tell you because I didn't want to lose you."

As I was fighting his hands from around my waist, he was gripping harder with tears falling down his eyes, and I started to cry into my hands.

David then started to unbutton my pants while looking up to me, still down on his knees. And I tried stopping him, but he pushed my hands out of the way.

He pulled my pants and panties down and started sucking on my clit. And as much heartache I was in for these past couple of days, he made me feel good. Gripping the back of his head with both of my hands, my eyes rolling in the back of my head, I was calling his name out softly.

"David, stop," I kept repeating, and with each lick and slurp he would mumble, "No."

Before I knew it, he was taking my clothes off and pulling me in the bathroom. He turned on the shower and started taking off his clothes while saying, "I'm sorry."

In my mind, I knew that I should have just called it quits and told that Negro to get the hell on. But instead, I was in the shower with him, bending over with water running down my back.

As he stroked in and out, it felt so good. He pulled out to cum. We stayed in the shower just for him to make me have another orgasm.

After climaxing for the second time, we got out of the shower and dried off. He then kissed me, apologizing again.

He got his clothes on. "I'm going to the funeral with your scent." Then he walked down the stairs, and I knew I had to get ready for the funeral myself, and a part of me really didn't want to go.

Chapter Eleven

"Ms. Guy," Dr. Martin said.

I looked up at the clock as I answered, "Yes."

"Looking back to that day, how were you feeling?" Dr. Martin asked.

"How was I supposed to have felt?" I snapped.

"Well, that's why I'm asking you," Dr. Martin responded while crossing his right leg over his left leg.

"I mean, I was angry, felt betrayed, sad, frustrated, mad, humiliated, every unhealthy emotion you can think of is what I felt."

My phone rung, and I knew who it was before looking at it. I sent my phone to voicemail and placed my phone in my purse.

"I guess I'll see you next Tuesday, Dr. Martin?" I said while raising up from the loveseat.

"Ms. Guy, does he make you happy?" Dr. Martin asked.

"Does it look like he does?" I asked, sarcastically with a fake smile.

"I'm only asking you because you're still with him."

I sat back down on the loveseat. "How do you figure I'm with him?"

"Well, he calls you around the same time every Tuesday, and when he calls, your whole demeanor changes," Dr. Martin replied.

I stood back up and walked towards the door. As I turned the knob and opened the door, I turned to Dr. Martin. "I think sometimes when you've been hurt and used so much by the one you love, you tend to turn into them. Same time next week?"

He answered, "Yes," and I closed the door behind me, exiting the building.

Chapter Twelve

As I reached the parking lot, Dr. Martin's car was already parked. It was 3:50 P.M., so I just waited until 4 o'clock to go into the building. I find Dr. Martin already sitting in his chair with his pen and notepad in hand, as I entered the room.

"Ms. Guy, how are you?" Dr. Martin asked while standing up to greet me.

"I'm okay, and you?"

"Absolutely fine."

I found my comfort spot on the loveseat, while Dr. Martin sat back in his chair, licking his finger and flipping through his notes in his notepad.

"We're at the part where you're going to attend Sherry's funeral or you didn't attend?" Dr. Martin asked.

"Aw yeah, the funeral-how can I ever forget?" I asked.

I was a little late arriving to the funeral, and the church was packed. I found a seat and was given an obituary. While reading through the obituary, I had come across David's name, which Sherry's family were acknowledging him as Sherry's special friend.

Dr. Martin could see my hurt because he tightened his lips and closed his eyes, shaking his head while listening to me. It wasn't until I paused when he opened his eyes and asked how I felt.

"My heart was punched at again, my stomach turned, and I just couldn't wait for the funeral to be over with," I replied.

"Now when the funeral was over, I left and went home just thinking, *What the hell.* I mean, shit like this is told on the 'Strawberry Letter' on the *Steve Harvey Morning Show.* I'm supposed to be hearing this, not living it!"

Dr. Martin got up to grab the Kleenex tissue box and handed it to me.

"Ms. Guy, I know it's hard reliving this, but talking about your past is beneficial because once the painful memories are out in the open, they begin to lose their power," Dr. Martin said. He sat beside me, patting my hand.

As I blew my nose into the tissue, every word Dr. Martin said made sense. I've never really told anybody how I truly felt. As a matter of fact, I usually pretend as if it never happened at times.

"Ms. Guy, after the funeral, how did you feel?" Dr. Martin asked.

"Well first thing - I was glad that it was over with. Secondly, I kept wondering why she would backstab me like that, because I would have never done that to her. Last but not least, how could I raise her twins?"

"Well, it seems as if you put the blame all on her and none on him."

"I would constantly remind David of their betrayal, especially during our arguments, Dr. Martin. But I was angry and mad at Sherry, and she wasn't even here to defend herself," I replied, and tears poured like a faucet down my cheeks.

"The first step is realizing and admitting, which is a good thing," Dr. Martin said.

He then closed the notepad and said, "Let's stop here."

I looked at the clock, and it was 4:20 P.M.. I was confused because he has never stopped me. It's usually me keeping up with the time.

"Okay," I said with an embarrassed look upon my face.

"Let's go for coffee," Dr. Martin said.

"Coffee?" I asked, smiling.

"Yes, coffee," he repeated, smiling back at me.

"Um..."

"Come on, Ms. Guy, not on a business level, but a friendship level."

"Okay, I guess I could," I replied.

"Great, there's a coffee shop just a few blocks away," Dr. Martin responded.

I grabbed my purse and waited for Dr. Martin to grab his belongings, schedule next week's visit, turn off lights, and then we both exited the building.

Chapter Thirteen

We parked side-by-side in the parking lot of But First Coffee, and as we got out of our cars, the wind was starting to pick up. The building was small, and the yellow paint was chipping off badly, which kind of made me wonder to myself why we went to this coffee shop of all places.

There was a chalkboard that read *Coffee Menu: Know Your Coffee* with lists of different brands of coffee.

"So what do you think?" Dr. Martin asked, as he led me up the shop's stoop.

"It's okay," I replied.

As he pushed open the door and held it open for me to enter, a bell above the door rang. A guy with a maroon apron was wiping down a table with a washcloth.

"Welcome to But First Coffee Shop," the worker said while still looking down wiping the table.

"Now is that how you greet people? Yo' mama taught you better than that," said Dr. Martin.

I turned to Dr. Martin thinking, *Oh my goodness, how rude of him.* That's when I heard the guy drop his washcloth onto the table, and I just knew it was about to go down in this coffee shop.

As I sensed the guy in the maroon apron start walking towards us, I couldn't help but to look. And as I turned, I saw the guy smiling from ear to ear with his arms out saying, "Maaaaannn, don't you scare me like that.

After the bad news I just got, I was gonna let you have it." He hugged Dr. Martin, and all you could hear was laughter and back smacking.

"So, what brings you by, boss? Who's this beautiful young lady?"

"Aw, yes, um," Dr. Martin said while clearing his throat.

"This is Meagan. She's a friend of mine." He was smiling.

"Meagan, this is Tony, he's been my best friend since we were kids."

As I reached my right hand out to shake Tony's hand, he raised it up to his lips and kissed my hand and said, "It's a pleasure to meet you."

I smiled and replied, "Same here."

"Okay, boss," Tony said while jumping straight to business mode and guiding Dr. Martin and me to a table for two.

The table was directly in front of a window, which had a beautiful street view.

"What can I get you two?" Tony asked with a pen and paper in hand.

"I'll take the cappuccino," Dr. Martin answered. Then they both looked at me.

Think, Meagan, think.

"I'm not really a coffee person, so I don't know," I embarrassingly replied.

Tony then replied, "Well, we have cappuccino, espresso, café latte, Americano, hot chocolate, tea-"

"I'll take hot chocolate," I interrupted.

"Cappuccino and hot chocolate coming up," Tony said while walking away.

"So that's your best friend, huh?" I asked Dr. Martin.

"Yeah. We've been best friends for over twenty years," Dr. Martin replied.

"Let me ask you a question, Meagan," Dr. Martin asked while removing his black scarf from around his neck.

"Yes," I replied.

"What do you like to do?" Dr. Martin asked.

I paused because as simple as the question was, I really don't know.

"Dr. Martin, I don't-"

"Please call me Carlton, Meagan," Dr. Martin insisted.

"Ooookaaaaay," I said, a little shocked.

"Okay. What did you like to do?" Dr. Martin asked while looking over at Tony who was walking over to us with our coffee teacups. I waited until Tony placed our cups in front of us and thanked him before I continued our conversation.

"Loved dancing, listening to music, writing, being around people, swimming, reading books, watching movies at the theatre, helping people, meeting new people, singing, playing basketball, playing video and board games, playing cards…" I paused. "…That's all I can think of right now."

Dr. Martin looked at me with a smile.

"What?" I asked, smiling.

"Nothing," Dr. Martin answered.

"Yes it is. So, why did you ask?" I asked.

"Nothing, for real, I think you just needed to hear and remind your own self of what you love to do," Dr. Martin explained.

My eyes widened, and my heart felt a little lighter because he was absolutely right. I had forgotten who I really am. I just smiled at him, and then my phone rang.

"You know this is my cue to go," I said.

"Tony!" Dr. Martin yelled.

"Yes," Tony answered while walking towards the table.

"I'm about to go, and tomorrow we'll link up," Dr. Martin responded, and they gave each other a brotherly hug.

Tony then reached for my hand and kissed it again, "It's been a pleasure meeting you, Meagan."

"Thank you and same here," I said, blushing.

Dr. Martin walked me to my car.

"Thank you Dr. - I mean Carlton, I really appreciated this," I said.

"No, you really needed that. I could tell from our first session, Meagan."

He opened my car door, and I got in, started my car, and watched him walk over to his car. Before he could even get his door open, I rolled down the passenger-side window and said, "By the way, I love your coffee shop. You don't seem like the type to have one."

He smiled and asked, "How did you know?"

"Oh, I forgot to tell you. I have psychic powers, too," I teased, and drove off, leaving him smiling from ear to ear.

Chapter Fourteen

As I pulled up to my sixth session, I was nervous and anxious, due to going to Dr. Martin's coffee shop. I must admit that he had been on my mind. I haven't felt like this in years, and I must say I like this feeling. I know when I walk through this door it's strictly business.

I walked through the door, and there he was waiting in his chair with his pen and notepad in hand.

"Good afternoon, Ms. Guy," Dr. Martin said.

"Hey," I replied while finding my way to the loveseat.

"So how are you feeling today?"

Oh, shit, he's good. He's strictly about business, and I like that. Why couldn't David have been like him?

"Oh, I'm fine. Thanks. And you?" I asked.

"I can't complain." He smiled, showing those pretty, straight white teeth.

"So we left off with you talking about Sherry's funeral. So you and David continued talking right?" Dr. Martin asked.

"Correct, and we eventually had a son of our own, named Alex."

"I'm all ears," Dr. Martin replied, looking surprised.

Chapter Fifteen

Well, David and I were starting to work on our relationship. I was working second shift, which was 3-11P.M., and David would work 7 A.M. to 11 P.M. somedays at his other job, which was down the street from my job. When he got off from work, he would pick me up from my job. Then we would go pick up his twins from the sitter, Lucy.

I would stay in the car while he would go in the sitter's house to get his twins. After we got to his place, we would take turns showering because he had some hollering babies. One of the twins was big, and the other was small. The small twin was the one to really cry the most, so what we did was I took one and he took the other. When it was bedtime, whenever the big twin awakened, it was I to fix his bottle to feed him, burp him, and change him. Whenever the small twin would cry, it was David's turn, but I would find myself waking up just to wake up David. He wouldn't wake up, so I would end up feeding, burping, and changing him too.

"So where was your daughter?" Dr. Martin asked.

"My sister was staying with me, so she helped me by keeping her so that I could help David some nights," I replied.

Dr. Martin nodded for me to continue.

I remember one morning David was supposed to go to work - at least, that's what he told me. That day a lady had come to his house and deep down inside, my woman's intuition was telling me that he was screwing her and that she was helping him, too, with his twins.

I went to work that afternoon, and David had picked me up at 11 P.M., and a mutual friend of David and I saw me getting picked up in his car. This coworker had also had two jobs and worked with David at her other job that was down the street.

The next day, when she saw me, she asked me if I was talking to David.

Um, duuuhhhh, I thought. "Yes we talk," I answered.

"Meagan, he talks to this girl named Tanya at our job," she said.

"What?!" I shouted.

I called him up on my phone in front of her, and he answered, "Hello."

"Who the fuck is Tanya?" I yelled through the phone.

"Tanya who?"

"Negro, don't act dumb - Tanya, the girl at your job, that Tanya!" I continued yelling into the phone.

"It's nothing between me and her."

"Don't worry, I'll be speaking to her myself because I'm not going through this shit with yo' ass again."

To my surprise he replied, "Go right ahead."

I hung up. My blood pressure was high, and I swear I saw nothing but red. I looked over to my coworker who had heard the whole conversation on speaker and told her to give Tanya my number so she could call me. Then I walked off to work.

A few hours later, my phone rang. "Hello," I answered to the unfamiliar number.

"Yes, this is Tanya. Is this Meagan?" she asked.

"Yes," I replied.

"How long have you been talking to my man?" she asked.

This bitch has her damn nerves to call me talking about her man. I was stunned.

"Your man?" I chuckled. "Yeah, he's your man now 'cause I just broke up with his ass. Oh, and since he's your man, call his ass up and ask him," I said, then hung the phone up.

How fucking rude of her. Here I thought we could come together and get his ass, and here this bitch is calling me disrespecting me. If you're trying to get any information from anyone, rule number one is that you shouldn't try to get smart.

I finished my shift in heartache but got through. It was really over between David and me, and I refused to give him another chance.

Here it is. I fell for a monster, and at this point, I wished I'd never met him. A couple of days went by with him begging me and still denying Tanya. As much as I couldn't stand the bitch that I've never met, I believed her.

I started feeling more tired, but I was working a lot since David was out of town. That's when I realized I was late coming on my menstrual period.

I brought a pregnancy test at a dollar store and prayed to God, "Let me not be pregnant."

I got home and ran straight to my bathroom, sat on the toilet, and peed on the pregnancy stick. I placed the test on the sink and washed my hands nervously. It felt like my heart was pounding out of my chest. I dried my hands, picked up the pregnancy test, and noticed two pink lines, reading positive.

"I'm pregnant," I whispered to myself, as I laid the test back on the sink.

Chapter Sixteen

"So, Ms. Guy, how did you feel after knowing you were pregnant?" Dr. Martin asked.

"I was sad, embarrassed, ashamed, and scared due to me being pregnant by a guy who I thought I knew. Then a part of me was happy and excited because here it was almost four years later after the loss of my stillborn son, and I was able to still have children. I mean, for all these years, I was thinking God punished me by taking away my son. Now here I am pregnant by someone I just found out had kids with a supposed friend of mine, and now I just found out he was in a relationship with someone else. Please, Lord, tell me this isn't who you had in mind for me to have a child with."

Dr. Martin looked at me, and I just knew he thought I was crazy, so I just stopped venting.

"Um, Ms. Guy, are you okay?" Dr. Martin asked.

Minutes had passed without me saying a word, and it was so silent that you could hear the hand of the clock move with each tick.

"Yeah, I'm okay. I just know you don't feel me. You don't get how I feel, and I'm not crazy, but as selfish as I may sound, I truly felt this way," I explained.

"Oh, no, Ms. Guy. Please don't ever think that. We as human beings question God and are upset with things in life. That's why the Bible says in Jeremiah 29:11, 'For I know the plans I have for you, declares the Lord, plans to prosper you and not harm you. Plans to give you hope and a future.'"

I must admit, I was surprised.

"So, Ms. Guy, God already knew that we would question Him. That's why He said these things, so we could read His words and know that He will never make a mistake. We just can't see in the future to know why things happen. That's why we're supposed to walk by faith, and not by sight. Now continue," Dr. Martin said.

I shifted on the loveseat to get comfortable with Dr. Martin staring at me. I then continued.

"I'm pregnant, David, and I don't think I'm gonna keep it," I said over the phone.

There was silence for a minute. Then David replied, "I don't want you to abort it, Meagan, please don't."

At this time, I was still not with David, and I was confused. It had been nine years since I had my daughter, Haylen, so I was definitely starting all over again.

David would say, "Meagan, let's move in together and get married." You know everything that sounded nice. Deep down inside, I knew it wasn't genuine, not after everything that has happened.

"I'll have to think about it, David," I said to him.

Dr. Martin asked, "Ms. Guy, so has David returned back from out of town?"

"Oh no. David was still in Baltimore with his twins supposedly over his brother's house."

"Oh, so David hasn't returned yet from the time you found out about Tanya?" Dr. Martin asked.

"Right," I responded.

It was Mother's Day shortly after that, and Vince, and my other good friend Nicole, and I were going out to celebrate. Vince wanted to stop to get some weed from an ex-coworker of ours who sold it. She was cool or what not, she was gay, and when we went up to her apartment, I ran into one of David's ex-girlfriends. She spoke then I spoke.

"Is this Tanya, the same woman who had called you?" Dr. Martin asked.

I chuckled, "No, me and my friends called her Dirty Di, short for the song named "Dirty Diana" by Michael Jackson," I replied.

Dr. Martin chuckled, "Dirty Di it is," then jotted notes down in his notepad.

"Well Dirty Di asked me if I had talked to David, and I told her yes, and that's when she went on about how he was calling her and how he wants to move in with her."

"Hold up. This man is out of town, and you find out he's messing with a coworker of his. Then you find out you're pregnant, and then he's trying to move in with another woman?" Dr. Martin asked while glancing through his notes.

I lowered my head and answered, "Yes."

Dr. Martin just shook his head.

While she's spilling the beans, my friend Nicole is tapping my leg on the low, as if saying, "Why she feels the need of telling you all this," and I'm just looking at Dirty Di listening, but nodding my head yes to Nicole, letting her know I feel her.

Vince being the guy he is said, "Well, Meagan is pregnant and is thinking about having an abortion." Nicole and I looked at Vince like "shut your mouth."

"Oh no, Meagan. Don't have an abortion. You can give the baby to me," Dirty Di said.

"Well, if you knew who it was by, then you would want her to have an abortion," Vince said.

"Vince!" Nicole and I both shouted at the same time.

"It's time to go, Vince!" Nicole said while raising up from the couch.

We got up and we walked out the house, after saying our goodbyes, and as soon as the door closed behind us Nicole said, "Biiiiiiittttttttttccccc-chhhhhh! What the hell was her problem?"

"I know, right? I guess she wanted to let me know David was still trying to be with her," I replied.

"Dirty Di is just jealous," Vince said, as we got into his car.

Vince and Nicole were talking about what just happened, and here it was I felt ashamed that my heart had just broken into two.

How could he do this to me? I thought to myself, trying to keep my cool and not look hurt. I suggested that we go to a gay club downtown, and Vince was super excited, so on our way to the gay club we went.

Chapter Seventeen

As I looked up at the clock, it was 5:30 P.M..

"Dr. Martin, oh my, it's been one and a half hours," I said, smiling.

"Don't worry, Ms. Guy, it's only been an hour," he said with a wink. "Besides, you have a lot built up in you that you need to let out," Dr. Martin added.

"Let me ask you this, Ms. Guy. Who have you ever talked to about what happened to you, and how you felt at that moment, and how you still feel about the situation?" Dr. Martin asked.

I looked up at him and nodded. "Dr. Martin, I hate reliving this part of my life with David. But you're right, I need to let it out."

I reached in my purse and grabbed my smartphone, which was set on silent, only to see I had five missed calls from David. As I turned my ringer on, stood, and started walking towards the door, Dr. Martin called my name. I turned around to look at him, and he was directly in front of me, and he gave me a hug so tight that all I could do was break down and cry.

"It's okay, Ms. Guy. You're a strong woman. You are telling me how a man has hurt you, and you're still standing strong. Not too many women are as strong as you," Dr. Martin said, then he let me go.

I wiped my nose with the back of my right hand and said, "Thank you."

As I turned around to turn the door knob, Dr. Martin said, "Ms. Guy, tonight's assignment is to read and remember Psalm 34:18 and Psalm 147:3."

"Okay," I said while opening the door.

Chapter Eighteen

It was exactly 4 o'clock when I pulled in the parking lot. I saw Dr. Martin's beautiful Mercedes, so I knew he was inside waiting for me. As I entered the room, I didn't see Dr. Martin, which was strange.

"Dr. Martin!" I called out, only for no response. I found my way to the loveseat, confused, wondering where Dr. Martin could have been or if anything had happened to him. That's when the door swung open, and all I could see was Dr. Martin holding a present in his hands. He then turned around to wave goodbye to someone in a car and then closed the door.

"Did I startle you?" Dr. Martin asked with a smile that brightened the whole room.

"No," I lied with a smirk.

"Sorry I'm a little late. That traffic came from nowhere," he said. Dr. Martin then walked over to hand me the small red wrapped present with a white bow on the top.

"Aw, you shouldn't have," I said with both of my hands reached out.

As I took the gift, Dr. Martin walked over to his coat rack to hang up his coat and scarf. I couldn't help myself, but damn he's fine. He walked over to his chair and as usual grabbed his pen and notepad then sat down in his chair.

I sat the present on the glass table in front of me and waited for him to tell me where we left off. Flipping through his notepad, he says, "We left off where Dirty Di had told you that David and her were talking on the phone." Dr. Martin then looked at me to start talking.

"Okay, basically we went out, and I really tried my best to act as if I was having a good time, but really I wasn't. Her words lingered in my head, and I was disgusted!"

"So did you confront David or did you just let it go?" Dr. Martin asked.

"Hell naw, I ain't let that shit go," I snapped. "David called me, and I let him have it," I added.

I swear I believe Dr. Martin was just all into my crazy love drama story, as if it were addicting, each session for him to find out more and more. I wonder if Dr. Martin ever felt that he couldn't wait for Tuesdays at 4 o'clock to come?

"Come to find out as soon as we left from our ex-coworker's house, Dirty Di called David to tell him she had just seen me. I knew David wasn't lying because he named the two people I was with, who were Vince and Nicole. I did tell him that I couldn't believe that he asked Dirty Di to move in with her, and of course, David denied it. I just knew deep down he was lying."

"Meagan, I want to be with you and live with you," David pleaded over the phone.

"David, you shouldn't have even been talking to her on the phone. So since you are talking to her, maybe that's who you should live with!" I yelled through the phone, before hanging up.

"So you told David to move with Dirty Di?" Dr. Martin asked, shockingly.

"Well, yeah. Why should I have a man living with me who's clearly having conversations with other women, and knowing deep down inside he asked this woman after knowing I'm pregnant to move in with her? So, hell yeah, that's where his ass needed to be."

Dr. Martin looked at me like I'm a different person because now I have an attitude.

"Did I think David was going to do exactly that? NO!" I added, after I calmed myself down.

"Well, Ms. Guy, what did you expect for David to do?" Dr. Martin asked.

"I expected for him to get his shit together. I expected for him to prove himself to me that he was truly in love with me. And If you're truly in love with anyone, you would do whatever it takes to do right by them … And boy was I wrong," I sighed.

Chapter Nineteen

David got back in town and moved in with Dirty Di, and I'm about four months pregnant. Looking back, I felt embarrassed, humiliated, stupid, angry, sad, disgusted, shit any negative emotion, I felt it.

I continued to work. As soon as I found out I was having a boy, I started putting in layaways at K-Mart. I must say that David did help out with the layaways. I kind of went overboard with buying things, and I mean, my son wasn't going to need really anything.

"So, you say, David was helpful financially?" Dr. Martin asked.

"Well, just with the layaways. I mean, I paid my own bills. I never asked him for too much. I guess because I figured I shouldn't have had to. He knew what situation I was in. Apparently, he didn't care, and I had a daughter to take care of as well."

"I see, so how about experiencing the pregnancy with David although he was living with another woman?"

"Ugh," I sighed, as my shoulders dropped. I glanced over to the window as if I were looking through a time machine.

"I can't recall one time he ever, and I mean ever, came to a doctor's appointment with me," I said, as I wiped tears running down my face.

Dr. Martin got up from his chair and walked over to his computer desk and grabbed a box of Kleenex to bring over to me. He sat beside me, rubbing my back with one hand and giving me tissues with the other.

"Ms. Guy... I'm sooooo sorry. Look, whenever you feel like you don't want to come anymore, I clearly understand. Because every Tuesday I'm just waiting to hear something good for once about David. This is our seventh session, and I have not yet heard one good thing besides you telling me that you and him are expecting a son." Dr. Martin was teary-eyed himself. "Of course, I'm not suggesting that you stop coming because reliving the past is painful, but only come if talking about it helps you."

I just nodded, and minutes later, after silence had passed, I said, "When I was about six months pregnant, I found out from a friend that Tanya was pregnant by David as well. She was having a girl, and we both were just weeks apart from one another."

"That must have been the hardest thing to take in with this pregnancy, I'm guessing," Dr. Martin said.

I inhaled then exhaled deeply. "Um, I really don't know. There was a time when I was at work, must I remind you that I was whispered about through the halls and residents' rooms. So dealing with that, I hated it there. One day, I was called to train an orientee. She seemed nice and had been a nurse aide way longer than me, so I really didn't find any need to train her. She would ask me questions about my pregnancy, such as how far along I was and what I was having. And of course, me being me, I was running off my mouth only to find out a few weeks later that she was living with David and Dirty Di."

"Wow, Ms. Guy. How did you manage to handle all the blows to your face? Every time you turn around there's something else. I mean, let's face it, the Devil was surely taunting you for a reason," Dr. Martin said.

"Yeah, I just kept praying, and besides there were some good people in that workplace," I said, as grabbing my purse and gift because it was 5 o'clock.

"What do you mean there were good people there at your job?" Dr. Martin asked.

"Let's just say a lot of people thought I got fired, but in reality, I was laid off at seven months pregnant. I could draw unemployment so that I could enjoy my baby until I was ready to come back. The agreement was that I couldn't tell anyone," I said while smiling all the way out the door.

Chapter Twenty

As I walked into the cozy warm office, Dr. Martin was already in position with his pen and notepad in hand, in his chair.

"Hello," I said while making my way to the loveseat.

"Hello, Ms. Guy," he replied.

"First, let me tell you that I appreciate the Joyce Meyer's *Life in the Word Devotional* book. It's very informative and helps me out spiritually," I said.

"I thought it would have been nice for you to have and that it would help you through your times of darkness. I even have one for myself, believe it or not," Dr. Martin said.

"Well, thank you again. I really appreciate it. And before we start, I believe I had an assignment to remember - Psalm 34:18 and Psalm 147:3 - and we were so into about the good people at my job that time had snuck up on us, and you didn't remind me."

"You're right, Ms. Guy, you now have my undivided attention," Dr. Martin said with a glow on his face, grinning from ear to ear.

"Psalm 34:18 - 'The Lord is close to the brokenhearted and save those who are crushed in spirit.'"

Dr. Martin looked excited, yet surprised. "That's right, 'The Lord is close to the brokenhearted and saves those who are crushed in spirit,'" Dr. Martin said while smiling.

I just smiled while shaking my head, "Psalm 147:3 - 'He heals the brokenhearted and binds up their wounds.'"

"Okay, Ms. Guy. You've done well. I'm proud of you. Just keep those two scriptures in mind, and everything will be okay."

"So, Ms. Guy, about the orientee living with David and Dirty Di, did you ever ask him about it?" Dr. Martin asked.

"Of course, and he admitted to it, but claimed he slept in the living room, which I knew was total bullshit," I replied.

I continued going to my doctor's appointments by myself. How could this be, though, I thought, day-in and day-out? What did I do to deserve this? Why is God keeping this baby and not my first son? I mean, Jason wasn't as bad of a man as David.

David would come over to my place, and of course, I would have sex with him most of the times. And I know that was stupid of me. Then the final day came when Alex was on his way to enter into this world.

Chapter Twenty-One

On December 11, 2012, I had an 8 lb. 14 oz., 21 ½ inch long baby boy, and I instantly fell in love. He was so, so handsome. He looked like he was a white woman's baby, and I didn't care. I just stared at him just looking - like out of all the bullshit I'm going through, I still had a handsome, healthy baby boy. I knew I was going to love him no matter what.

My mother was the only one at the hospital when it was time for delivery. Everyone had come and left before I had the baby. After all, I was in labor for about 30 hours.

My family and friends had come to visit me and baby Alex. When we were placed in our room, David came by the next morning. He just looked at the baby. I believe because the baby looked white, but he didn't question me. He stayed for a few hours and held the baby, helped change him, took pictures, and then all of a sudden, "I guess I better be going," David said. I knew he had snuck over to the hospital, and he didn't have his twins, so I knew Dirty Di must have been keeping them.

I wondered what lie he told her to get away to come to the hospital. He gave Alex a kiss on his forehead and left the room. I really can't tell you how he seemed to feel - if he was happy or not - but I really didn't care how he felt. I just knew I was the happiest person in the world at that moment, and I couldn't worry about him. I have a newborn who needs for me to stay strong for him, not to mention my daughter, Haylen, too.

The next morning, I was getting our belongings, ready to go home. We were going to be discharged around noon, and my mother had picked me and Alex up from the hospital.

Entering into my home with Alex was a new, fresh beginning - not only for me but also for Haylen and Alice. It was a new adjustment, I mean, from having just us three to now living with a newborn, which was hectic. It took months for us all to settle down into a steady routine. David had his few days out of the week that he would come over and spend time with me, because the baby was always sleeping, and he rarely had his twins, which only made me think that he was sneaking over to my place.

His daughter was born, and he never talked about her because he was still denying the fact that he could be the child's father. Bullshit is what I always thought and said.

David must have really missed his real family because when Alex was three months old, he pulled up to my house excited. "Meagan, come. I have a house I want y'all to come check out with me!" David said, very excitedly.

"What house?" I asked, anxiously.

"It's down the road from you, close to both of our jobs!" he explained, still excited with his car keys in his hand.

"Okay, we got to get dressed!" I said, and rushed up my stairs.

David was really happy. He followed behind me, and while I was getting dressed, he dressed the baby and put him in his baby car seat. I grabbed Alex's diaper bag, and we headed out the door.

"I think you're gonna like it," David said while buckling the baby in the car.

We both got in the car at the same time and put our seatbelt on. David started the car, and off we went.

He stopped in front of a beautiful brick house, literally just a few minutes away from my house. The house had a beautiful shade tree in the front yard, and oh, how big the yard was front and back. The house had a driveway and an open garage, and while looking at this house, it kind of reminded me of the "Golden Girls" home.

"Let's go inside," David said while pulling out the house key.

David got out, walked up the driveway to open the door, ran back to the car to grab Alex out of his baby car seat, and headed back to the house. I followed.

My eyes widened, as I started walking through the beautiful, cozy house. The living room was huge with shining, dark brown hardwood floors that was attached to the walk-through kitchen, which you could enter into from the bedroom hallway or the living room.

What caught my attention in the kitchen was that it had a stove on one side, beside the kitchen sink, and directly across from the sink was the oven that was attached to the wall. I'd never seen that layout before.

The house had three bedrooms, which really weren't that big, not even the master bedroom. So walking through the hall the first bedroom and the master bedroom were to the left, and the bathroom, which was also small, and another bedroom was to the right. It was perfect for David and the kids.

"What you think?" David asked.

"I love it!" I replied while hugging him and Alex.

"Me, too, that's why I got it. I'm ready to be with my family," David said, then kissed me.

Chapter Twenty-Two

Dr. Martin was sitting with his legs crossed with his pen and notepad on his lap. I'm starting to believe that I'm telling him a little too much. I mean, *What am I even doing here for real,* I thought to myself.

"So you were excited about the house?" Dr. Martin asked.

"Yes," I replied. Within a week he was going to be moving in. I called my job telling them I was ready to come back to work. Since I was fake fired, I had to put in another application along with having a background check and drug screen done. It had been a while since I'd worked, and as much as I loved spending time with Alex, I was ready to go back to work. After my background and drug test had come back, I was ready for orientation the following week.

"David, I need for you to watch Alex next Tuesday. I have orientation," I told him over the phone.

"Okay," he responded with no hesitation.

Tuesday came, and David was at my house bright and early. I was still getting ready for my orientation. Looking in my dresser mirror to put my eyeliner on, I asked David, "So how do I look?" turning around to face him. I had pink scrubs on with white Force's on.

"You look like you're ready to work the floor," he responded, laughing. "You know it's just paperwork today and tomorrow, and then you'll be working on the floor."

I rolled my eyes, then turned back around to put my brown lipstick on.

"Don't be hating."

Alex was wide awake laying on his tummy in his bassinet making baby noises. David picked him up and started talking to him.

"Hey, son, Mama is about to leave, so it's just going to be me and you," he said, and Alex had this look like "you really don't know me."

"Okay, David. The baby milk is on the kitchen counter, and the bottled water is in the kitchen pantry. Give him 6 ounces of water along with three scoops of the Good Start powder milk, okay?" I instructed.

"Meagan - okay, okay. I got this. Don't worry," he said while putting Alex back in his bassinet that was beside my bed.

David walked up to me, placed his hands around my waist. "We still have time."

"David, no," I said, backing away.

David then started kissing my neck, and it felt sooo good. Then we started French kissing. With one of his hands sliding down in my scrub pants, he gently caressed my clitoris. Then one finger entered inside of me, and I gasped while my eyes rolled in the back of my head. In and out, in and out, he repeated - then two fingers in and out, in and out. Then he turned me around and pulled my scrub pants down, and I bent over with my arms placed on my dresser. He was now unbuckling his pants, and then they dropped to his ankles. Holding his dick in his hand, he inserted it, and I said, "Wait. We need a condom!"

"You're not going to get pregnant, Meagan. And I'm not fucking no one but you. This is your dick," David whispered in my ear.

Before I knew it, David was stroking in and out, moaning.

"Meagan, I love you. Let's get married. Will you marry me, Meagan?" he asked.

It felt so good that I tried to hold my moan in because Alex was in his bassinet.

"David, I love you, I love you, I love you," I moaned.

"This is your dick," he said, and started pounding faster, and I could feel his dick getting ready to explode like a volcano, and as I said, "Don't cum inside of me!" it was too late.

"David, noooooo! I can't get pregnant right now!" I said, turning around to face him.

"You're not going to get pregnant," he replied. We both walked to the bathroom to wash off.

"Meagan, I meant everything I said," David said while pulling up his pants.

"I hear you," I said, as I walked out of the bathroom to check on Alex, who was now sound asleep. I bent down and gently kissed him on his cheek and headed downstairs.

"Have a nice first day of orientation, Mama," David said, following behind me.

"Well, thank you, Daddy," I said, and walked out the door.

Chapter Twenty-Three

Dr. Martin was glancing at me when I snapped back to reality. "It seems like you and David are getting along well," Dr. Martin says with a smile.

"Yes, this is the David I knew he could be," I replied. "This is all I wanted, for him to step up and be a man."

I went to orientation, everybody was glad to see me or, should I say, most acted as if they were happy. I had so many people to show pictures to of Alex on my phone during the breaks in orientation. Telling the birth weight and length repeatedly was exhausting, but each time I was excited.

It wasn't until Dirty Di's friend wanted to see a picture of Alex.

Meagan, curse her ass out! I thought. I hesitated and then pulled out my smartphone and showed her.

Dr. Martin's eyebrows rose, and he leaned forward as if he were watching a movie, waiting to see what's going to happen next.

That's when she said, "He looks like the small twin" and that my son was cute. And from that moment, I knew she was going to run back and tell her friend, and to be honest, I couldn't wait.

"Well, you know he moved?" she asked.

"Yeah, me and Alex were with him when he picked the house out," I replied.

"Yeah, he lives down the street," she said.

I didn't respond, but how my heart dropped, my facial expression probably showed that I was shocked to know that she would know.

When I got home, before I could even confront David, he met me at the door and told me he had a doctor's appointment for his twins tomorrow. He said that he wouldn't be able to watch Alex. As I sat on my couch with my elbows on my knees and my hands covering my face, I was now wondering who would watch Alex for me tomorrow while I went back to orientation.

It was 5 o'clock so I gathered up my belongings.

"I guess I'll see you next Tuesday," I said while walking towards the door.

"Of course," Dr. Martin said. "Have a nice evening, Ms. Guy."

"Same to you too."

Chapter Twenty-Four

Snow was heavily falling down, and I was contemplating rescheduling, which David insisted for me to do. But the more I thought about it, I decided to make that drive to vent to Dr. Martin.

As I walked through the door, I stomped my brown fur Coach boots on the welcome mat. The wind was so strong that snow had blown inside the office.

"Brr," I said while taking my brown pleated scarf off, along with my earmuffs and gloves.

"It's cold out there, isn't it?" Dr. Martin asked while sitting at his computer desk.

He had startled me because I didn't even notice him sitting there.

"Yes, it is," I replied, and took a seat on the loveseat.

Dr. Martin stood from his desktop computer and walked to his chair. As I watched him walk, all I could do was wonder if he was a good man or a dog like the ones I tend to attract.

He sat down in his chair and grabbed his pen and notepad as usual, and I said, "We're at the part where I had to find out who was going to watch Alex for me while I attended day two of my orientation."

"Okay," Dr. Martin said with a smile.

"Mama, I'll call Mama!" I said, and dialed her number.

Ring. Ring. Ring. "Hello," my mother answered.

"Mama, I started orientation today, and David came to watch Alex, and now all of a sudden he has a doctor's appointment to go to and-"

"And what the hell does that have to do with him not watching his son?" she interrupted. "I told you he was full of shit. Here it is you trying to go back to work, and he's already not trying to watch him," she added. "What time do you have to be there?"

"Well, I don't have to be there until 10 A.M.."

"I'll be at your house at 9:30. There's no need of you dragging that baby out in this cold. And have y'all even been to his house yet?"

"No. He's still trying to get settled in," I lied.

"That motherfucker probably moved that girl with him. I don't put nothing past his ass!"

As much as I hated hearing her talking shit about David, she had a point. We were never invited back to his house since the day he came to show us.

"Okay, Mama, thank you. I'll see you in the morning," I said, trying to rush her off the phone.

"How's Haylen and Alex?" she asked.

"They're okay. I'm waiting on Haylen to get off the bus now, and Alex is here sleeping," I replied.

"Is Alice still at work?"

"Yeah, she's working late today and tomorrow."

"Okay, see you in the morning."

"Okay, bye," I said, and we both hung up.

How much of a fool am I to let David keep doing this? I felt used. I just had unprotected sex with this man, and then he's making up excuses to not watch his son. I mean, the baby has been in this world for only three months, and his father has been full of shit way before he was born and still is.

I woke up at 7 A.M. to get Haylen ready for school, and Alex just laid on his back looking around at his surroundings smiling.

After I dressed for orientation, I got Alex's bottles ready with water, started laundry, and cleaned the house until my mother showed up. At 9:30 A.M., she was pulling up in front of my house, blowing her horn. I welcomed her in with Alex in my arms.

While she was reaching out for Alex she asked, "Have you talked to David since he left yesterday?"

"No," I replied, ashamed.

"I told you to take your time going back to work. Your job even told you to take as long as you like," she said, finding her way to my chocolate brown sectional couch.

I didn't feel like talking about this, so I changed the subject.

"Alex's bottles are already filled with water, and I put the Good Start on the kitchen counter next to them," I said.

"Where's the baby cereal?"

"He can't have baby cereal yet, Mama!"

"Shit. As big as his butt is, that milk ain't filling him up," she went on and on.

"Well, we will be getting out of orientation at 2:30 or 3 P.M.."

"And what about tomorrow?"

"It's from 10 A.M. to 2 P.M.."

"I guess I'll come back tomorrow same time 'cause I have a feeling he's not going to do it."

"Okay," I said, then kissed Alex on the cheek and headed out the door.

Chapter Twenty-Five

Weeks went by and David had not once come to watch Alex since the first day I went to orientation, and I couldn't afford daycare right now because I was working only PRN.

"What's PRN?" Dr. Martin asked.

"PRN is when you choose to work different available shifts offered," I replied.

I only did this because I didn't have a steady babysitter. My brother, Roz, watched Alex a few times for me, which would be second shift 3 to 11 P.M. because he had a daughter three weeks after Alex was born.

I say it was a month after I started working there when I went to my DON (Director of Nursing) with tears in my eyes. I told her that I had to quit because the father of my son had agreed to watch him during the week and has reneged on his word, and how I really didn't have a sitter.

Embarrassed, I felt my cheeks burning, and that's when she asked, "Well, have you thought about receiving welfare and going to school?"

I looked at her shocked, and I guess it showed.

"Well, about twenty years ago, I was in the same predicament, and I received welfare and went to school. That's how I'm a nurse to this very day," she explained.

"I just might," I said.

But knowing deep down in my heart that I wasn't, I just wanted to work!

We gave each other a hug, and I left the nursing home saddened and lost.

"Ms. Guy, so what was David doing at this time for him to not want to keep his son?" Dr. Martin asked with a puzzled look.

"David never really said nor gave a reason," I replied.

"Well, surely you went back to your unemployment?" he asked with a look saying, "Don't you tell me no."

"No," I said, dropping my head. "Every two weeks of free money. I sure damn missed it. I didn't even look back to drawing my unemployment again."

"How did you pay your bills?" Dr. Martin asked, concerned.

"Well, I was receiving food stamps and WIC, and my car was paid off. I was on Section 8, so my rent was based on my income. My mother, my sister, Alice, and my brother, Roz, would help me out with money for my electric, my phone and cable bill, and gas for my car."

My brother mostly helped out because my mom was on a fixed income. She was hurt on her job, so she was drawing her disability and retirement, so I didn't stress my bills to her. My sister, Alice, was living with me, so we always split the bills in half before this situation. I didn't expect for her to pay all the bills. She was working at a restaurant for minimum wage, and besides, it wasn't her responsibility. I made the decision to have this baby, so I now have to do what I have to do. And for the first time in my life I felt stuck.

My brother, Roz, and I were very close, although we were eight years apart. He made money on the side and helped us out tremendously, and I'm forever grateful because I don't know how I could have done it without those three financially. Now when it came to diapers, wipes, anything for the baby, David would provide. I would continue to put in layaways for Alex, and he would give me the money to pay towards it. So I started putting things for my daughter, Haylen, in layaway as well. And since he never wanted to see the receipts, he never had a clue.

"So your immediate family helped out with your bills, and David helped out with only the baby's needs, correct?" Dr. Martin asked.

"Correct."

Dr. Martin shifted back in his chair, shaking his head in disgust.

"Yeah, it wasn't until I realized I still haven't come on my period, and I was scared," I replied. *I cannot now be pregnant, God, not now, Lord,* I thought to myself as I looked down at the pregnancy test.

Chapter Twenty-Six

"David, I'm pregnant," I said, and there was a long silence on the other end of the line.

"Well, say something, dammit!" I demanded.

"You have to have an abortion," David replied.

My heart dropped. As badly as I didn't want to be pregnant, to hear him say those words were hurtful. I mean, it was him who insisted to have sex when I told him we needed a condom.

"I can't afford to have an abortion, David. I'm already struggling with these bills," I pleaded.

Dr. Martin looked stunned, and when I caught the surprised look on his face, he then looked down at his notes. There while shifting trying to find a comfortable place on the loveseat, I could tell that Dr. Martin was getting a little bit emotional because he asked, "So was he going to pay for it?"

"Well, he never volunteered to pay for me to have it done," I responded. "So I prayed to the Lord above telling Him that I messed up and that this baby was going to be too much for me to bear."

I kept this a secret for as long as I could, and then the baby sickness kicked in. This baby didn't like *anything*. I couldn't drink pop, couldn't eat out, and that drove me crazy. I finally ended up telling my brother, Roz, and my cousin, Latoya, my secret about being pregnant, and they swore not to tell a soul.

"Latoya must be a close cousin?" Dr. Martin asked.

"Yeah, I have a few close cousins, though," I responded.

"Latoya and Roz were around the same age. She had no kids of her own, but she helped everyone out in the family with their kids, like babysitting, and if you ever needed her, you could depend on her."

"What are you going to do, Meagan?" Latoya asked.

"I don't know!" I replied, pacing back and forth.

"Have you told David yet?"

"Hell yeah, he knows," I replied, rolling my eyes.

It was Alex's bedtime, so Latoya helped out with his bath, while I helped with Haylen's homework.

"Thank you, Latoya," I said, as she was gathering her belongings to head out the door.

"Aw, you're welcome, Meagan. I told you I'm here whenever you need me."

I watched as she drove off. Alex and Haylen were sound asleep when Alice got home from work, and I broke the news to her. She was happy to know that she was going to have another niece or nephew, but she was also saddened because David hasn't stepped up as a real father to Alex who needed him.

"Have you told Tina?" she asked.

"No, and I don't want you running yo' mouth and telling Mama either!" I demanded.

"I'm not, but you should tell her," Alice replied.

Alice was the tattletale of Roz and I. He and I would tell each other secrets, and right after we tell one another our secrets, it would always end with, "Don't tell Alice..."

My body was tired dealing with this pregnancy, dealing with Alex with his days and nights mixed up, and my morning and night sickness. The thought of aborting heavily weighed on my mind. A week has passed. I was bleeding, and I panicked. I had my mother watch Haylen and Alex as I went to the emergency room with my cousin, Latoya.

Nervous and scared at the same time because I had already experienced having a stillborn before, it brought back memories of that day.

At this time, Roz met up with us and walked in right before the doctor came in.

"Ms. Guy, I'm Dr. Osborne, and you're having a spontaneous abortion, which cannot be prevented. About 70% of women in their first trimester miscarry. Your HCG pregnancy levels are low, and the pelvic and abdominal ultrasound showed no sign of a baby. So, if there's any heavy bleeding occurring where you have to change two pads within an hour, please come back." She handed me my discharge papers.

"Here's a list of OB/GYN doctors you can choose from, along with their numbers, so you can call to schedule a follow-up appointment within 2-3 days." She left the room.

"Are you okay?" Latoya asked.

"Yeah. I'm okay, Latoya," I replied.

"You gonna be alright, Pappy," Roz said, and the three of us walked out of the hospital.

The drive, all the way back home after picking up Alex and Haylen from my mother's house, I was thinking, *I'm going through this miscarriage alone while David is living his life.*

Chapter Twenty-Seven

I picked up the discharge papers from my wooden dining room table. With the papers were a list of OB/GYN doctors suggested for a follow-up due to my miscarriage. I was drawn to a woman doctor by the name of Iris Wilson, so I picked up my cell phone and called the number.

"Hello. This is Dr. Iris Wilson's office. How may I help you?" the soft voice of the receptionist answered.

"Yeah, um, this is Meagan Guy, and I'm calling because I was seen at Saint Joseph Hospital last night. I'm having a miscarriage, so I'm calling to schedule a follow-up," I explained.

"Okay. I'll just need to gather some information from you, and I'll be glad to set up your appointment with Dr. Wilson."

"This must have been hard to deal with by yourself, huh?" Dr. Martin asked while jotting down notes in his notepad.

"Yeah, but I had to do what I had to do," I replied.

After giving the receptionist my name, social security number, home address, phone number, and insurance information, she then said, "We have an appointment available tomorrow at 2 o'clock P.M.. If that's not too soon for you, we have-"

"No, that'll be fine!" I interrupted.

"Okay. See you tomorrow at 2 o'clock P.M.," she said.

Pulling up to the doctor's office, I was scared and nervous. I got out of the car and walked into the building, taking a deep breath. There were two white receptionist women at the check-in counter.

"Hello. May I help you?" one of the receptionists asked.

"Yes, I have a 2 o'clock appointment with Dr. Wilson," I answered, nervously.

"I'll need for you to fill out this form. Do you have your ID and insurance card?" she asked while handing over a clipboard.

"Yes, ma'am," I said, pulling them both from my billfold wallet.

"Okay, just have a seat. I'll make copies of these and give them back to you when you finish your paperwork and bring it to me," she said, smiling.

I found a chair by the T.V. and started to fill out the forms. After I finished, I walked back up to the receptionist, and she handed me my ID and insurance card and told me I would be called shortly.

Minutes had passed, which felt like forever, then my name was called. I had greeted a nurse who was holding a clipboard. "Just follow me," she instructed, and I followed.

We walked past two doors, and the next room to the right was my room to be seen in.

We walked in, and she had me stand on a scale and took my weight.

"Okay. 105 pounds," she said. "Now let's stand over by the wall so I can get your height," she added. I did exactly what I was told.

"5' 5," she said while jotting down my information.

"She then left out the room and came back with a nurse on a stick."

"A nurse on a stick?" Dr. Martin asked, laughing.

"It's the vital sign monitoring equipment that has your blood pressure cuff, your oxygen reader, your heart rate, and pulse reader," I explained.

"Oh, okay. I see," Dr. Martin said, calming himself down from laughing.

She checked my vitals, and everything was okay.

"Now I need for you to follow me to the restroom," she said while holding out a cup.

"I need for you to urinate in this cup. When you're done, just place the cup in the silver cabinet and return back to the room, and Dr. Wilson will then be in to see you," she explained while showing her straight pearly white teeth.

"Okay," I said, and closed the door.

I pulled my pants down and squatted over the toilet seat then placed the cup under me and started peeing. I put the top on the cup, placed it in the cabinet, wiped, pulled my pants up, flushed the toilet, then washed my hands.

Entering the room, I was so anxious and nervous that my hands were sweating. Minutes later, the doctor walked in with the nurse.

"Hello, Ms. Guy. I'm Dr. Wilson, and I hear that you were at the emergency room two nights ago due to you having a spontaneous abortion. Is that correct?" she asked while glancing through some papers.

"Correct," I replied.

"Okay. Looking at your HCG pregnancy levels, they are now low, so I'm going to proceed to do a vagina and abdominal ultrasound to see if I can see anything. We're going to step out while you get undressed from the waist down. Just cover up with this sheet, and we'll return."

"Yes, ma'am," I replied.

As soon as the door closed shut behind them, I started taking off my shoes, pants and panties. I placed my belongings in a chair that was in the corner and climbed onto the examining table and placed both feet in the stirrups. I then placed the sheet over me.

A gentle knock was at the door before they entered the room with the ultrasound machine. The doctor had explained what she was about to do, and I just laid on my back, numb. Before I knew it, it was over with, and she told me I could put my clothes back on and that she would return soon to give me her findings.

As soon as the door closed, I rushed over to the chair and started putting my clothes and shoes on. It felt like forever for her to come back, but I patiently waited.

Knock. Knock. My heart, I swear, was pounding through my ears, my breathing got heavy, and my throat was dry.

"Ms. Guy, there's no baby. You've miscarried, which I'm sorry. You're HCG levels were low, but it's normal to read you're still pregnant after a miscarriage. Would you like any birth control?" Dr. Wilson asked.

Trying to not cry and show my emotions, I replied, "Yes."

"Well, we have several birth control options, which are the birth control pills, the NuvaRing, the Depo Shot-"

"I'll take the NuvaRing," I interrupted.

"That's a good choice. A lot of my patients love the NuvaRing," she said.

"I'm going to give you three months' worth of supplies. You just insert it into the vagina to provide birth control. It works like the pill but only needs to be inserted once a month. It will also come with instructions. Now, you will have to insert it in after you start your next menstrual period."

"Okay."

Dr. Wilson walked out for a brief moment and then returned with three NuvaRing packages. With my hand held out, I thanked her.

"In three months, I would like to see you. So when you check out, the receptionist will schedule your appointment," she said, then apologized again before exiting the room.

I then looked up to the ceiling and thanked God for answering my prayers. They say God won't put too much on you that you can't bear, and I guess He knew I couldn't handle having this baby due to the situation I was in.

Chapter Twenty-Eight

Weeks went by, and I was waiting for my period to come so I could insert the NuvaRing in. Meanwhile, David still had not invited us to his house. What a sad situation I was in. I mean, how can you live basically up the street from someone and not want to be bothered with your own child? He would come over two or three times a week for a few hours - more so to see me, I believe, than his own flesh and blood. I know, sickening.

Alex had turned six months. He was getting so big, and Haylen was enjoying every moment with him. That's when it hit me that a month had gone by, and I still hadn't started my period, so I could insert the NuvaRing. I went to the dollar store again by my house and brought two pregnancy tests. Anxiously, I drove all the way home praying.

"God, I haven't had sex since the last time David and I had sex, and the doctors said I had a miscarriage. Please let everything be okay with me!" I pleaded.

Pulling up in my driveway, I parked the car and hurried inside the house and ran straight to the upstairs bathroom. My heart was pounding, and everything seemed to be moving in slow mode as two light pink lines appeared on the test.

"This can't be!" I screamed.

Well, the doctor did say that my HCG levels would eventually go down, so maybe it's going down and still making me test positive for pregnancy. I needed someone to call so I called Nicole.

"What's up, girl?" Nicole asked, as she answered on the first ring.

"Girl, I haven't come on yet, and I just took a pregnancy test, and it's still reading positive!" I explained.

"So, you haven't had a period since the miscarriage?" Nicole asked.

"No," I answered.

"Meagan, do a walk-in at the Women's Pregnancy Center. They will do a test and an ultrasound. They will be able to tell you what's going on."

"Okay. Where is the place?" I asked.

"Right on Nicholasville Road, right across from the Central Baptist Hospital. You can't miss it. If you get lost, just call me, and I'll give you the directions."

"Thanks, girl. I'm about to head out now."

Pulling up to the brick red building, I started feeling sick to my stomach the closer I got to the entrance door. As I entered the building, I was greeted by a woman.

"I was told that you all do a pregnancy test, and I was wondering if I could have one done?" I asked.

"You've come to the right place. Just sign in and check what services you're needing," she replied.

I signed in and sat down in a chair next to the door. The room was comfortable, warm, and there was soft classical music playing, which helped ease my mind.

"Meagan Guy," a gray-haired lady said with a clipboard in her hand.

"Yes," I answered while standing up.

"Hello, I'm Julie, the nurse here. If you follow me, I'll take you to the restroom so you can urinate in this cup."

I followed her.

When I finished, I washed my hands, and as I opened the door, Julie was waiting there with latex gloves on.

"Now, if you would go back to the front and wait, it'll be a few minutes for me to give you the results," she said with a smile.

I walked to the waiting room, and now I'm starting to feel sick to my stomach. About 5 minutes later, Julie called my name, and I must admit that seemed to be the longest 5 minutes of my life.

"Yes," I replied.

"Follow me," she said.

We both entered a room with ultrasound equipment, and on the wall was a flat screen T.V.. A lady then walked in wearing a white lab coat, greeting me with her hand out, she said, "I'm Dr. Woods. Congratulations! You're pregnant."

I'm pretty sure my facial expression was like, "WHAT THE HELL?"

"Can you tell me when your last menstrual period was?" Dr. Woods asked.

"Well, Dr. Woods, I'm not supposed to be pregnant," I answered, and the doctor looked at me confused.

"Well, I went to the emergency room a few months ago, and they said I was having a spontaneous abortion. Then two days after that, I went to a different doctor for a follow-up, and that doctor confirmed that there was no baby by using an ultrasound as well. I was waiting to start my menstrual period so that I could insert my NuvaRing in, but I never started my period," I explained.

"I'll need to perform an ultrasound on you, so if you would lie back on the examination table and pull up your shirt, let's take a look," Dr. Woods said.

I did exactly what she instructed me to do. I closed my eyes as she walked over to the sink to wash her hands then put some gloves on. The nurse brought in some towels.

"Now, this is going to be a little cold," Dr. Woods explained, as she placed the gooey liquid gel on my stomach.

With my eyes still closed, I felt the ultrasound stick rubbing across my stomach. As she paused to take pictures, she then said, "Here's your baby - looks like you're twelve weeks!"

I opened my eyes to see this little human being on the television screen. Though glad to know that I wasn't going crazy, I had already had my mind made up. I was going to have an abortion.

Chapter Twenty-Nine

I believe the doctor and nurse could tell I wasn't happy at all about the news because I was sent into a small room with posters of smiling babies of all different races. A brown table beside me had a Bible and a box of Kleenex placed on it. A blonde lady then walked in the room.

"Hello, Meagan. I'm Robyn, the counselor here," she said.

"Hello," I said, still looking sad.

"So I heard about you being told that you had miscarried, now you're seeing that you're twelve weeks pregnant!" she said, smiling.

"Correct," I replied.

I think my body language told her that I was disappointed at the results because that's when she walked over to the room across the hall and came back with a brown box. This brown box was similar to the game called Mancala. She opened the box, and there were small rubber babies at different stages, week by week, during the three trimesters while in the mother's womb.

"Here's what your baby's stage looks like right now. The baby has its toes and fingers and has a heartbeat!" she explained.

I must say I was sad at the fact that I'm even thinking about aborting my child, and I busted out crying in tears. Robyn then grabbed the box of Kleenex from off the brown table and handed me a few tissues.

I started telling Robyn about my situation with David. She was then sitting next to me with tears in her eyes as I was explaining how an abortion is what I had to do.

"Dear Heavenly Father, please wrap your arms around Meagan, and help her with her situation, Lord. Please come into her heart and like you said in Psalm 127:3 , 'Children are a heritage from the Lord, offspring a reward from Him.' Please be with Meagan, Lord, and show her everything will be alright. Help her to have faith because all she needs is you and everything will be alright, in Jesus' name."

"Amen," we both said at the same time.

I must admit that I felt a little bit better, and when walking out of the building, my faith was uplifted, and the Lord knew that was what I really needed.

Chapter Thirty

David was entering through my door when I was feeding Alex. Haylen was at school, and Alice was at work.

"So what's up?" David asked.

I walked over to the kitchen table, still feeding Alex.

"What's wrong, Meagan?" David asked, as he walked over to me.

Two of the ultrasounds were lying face up on the kitchen table.

"What's this?" David asked while reaching for the ultrasounds.

"So you're going to get pregnant by another man?" he yelled, staring straight at me with anger.

By this time, Alex is crying because David had startled him. Bouncing the baby up and down and trying to burp him I asked, "What?"

"You're fucking other men and bringing them around my son?" David yelled again.

"No, I never had a miscarriage apparently," I said, trying to get the baby under control.

"How is that possible when the doctors told you there was no baby in your stomach?" David asked while reaching out for crying Alex.

"I have no fucking idea!" I replied. "I'm still trying to wrap my head around this!"

"Well, you have to get rid of it," he said.

I didn't respond, and I went upstairs to myself so he could finish his few hours of Daddy and son time with Alex. When he got Alex to sleep, he brought him upstairs and laid him in his bassinet.

"I'm about to go," David said. As he turned to go down the stairs, he added, "We can't afford another child right now."

"Yeah, I know," I replied.

Ring. Ring. Ring.

"Yeah, Pappy," my brother, Roz, answered.

"I'm pregnant still!" I told him.

"Girl how? The doctors said you were having a miscarriage."

"Yeah, I know, but I never came back on! I'm thinking maybe it was too soon for the baby to show because I went to this one place that gives pregnancy tests and ultrasounds, and they confirmed I was about twelve weeks."

"Okay. What you gonna do?" Roz asked.

"I want to have an abortion, but I don't have the money."

"I got you, so when you gonna make an appointment?"

"Well, I have to this week because I'm already twelve weeks, and they stop doing abortions here at twelve weeks. I would then have to go outta town to have it done."

"Okay. Call and let me know."

"Okay, but don't tell Mama or Alice."

"You know I ain't," he replied, before hanging up.

I then googled the abortion clinic's number and called them.

"Women's Abortion Clinic - this is Kelley. How may I help you?" the lady answered.

"Yes, this is Meagan, and I'm calling to schedule an appointment with y'all."

"Okay. We will perform an ultrasound to make sure you're not over twelve weeks pregnant, and if you're not, the abortion procedure is $600. You will also need to bring someone 18 years or older with a valid driver's license. They will need to drop you off and pick you up due to you being on pain medicine and not being able to drive."

"Yes ma'am. That'll be fine."

"So how about tomorrow?" Kelley asked.

I'm already twelve weeks, so Meagan you better, I thought to myself. "That's fine."

"Come at 9 A.M.. There may be protestors out. Don't pay them no mind. They cannot come on our property, and there will be a police officer in his car parked on the main road in front of our building."

She gave me the address, and we hung up. I called Roz back and told him the cost and how the appointment was going to be the very next day.

"Coo'. I'll bring you the money in the morning."

"Okay. Thank you."

"Yep," he replied.

I ended up calling my friend Gina. Gina and I had been good friends for a while. We met at Frenchburg Job Corps back in 2002. We became good friends after we had finished there.

"Hello, friend," Gina answered.

"I need a favor Gin-Gin."

"Yeah, what's up?" Gina replied.

"I need to spend the night out there-"

"You know y'all always welcomed."

"Yeah, but I need for you to drop me off at the abortion clinic and pick me back up and keep Haylen and Alex while I'm there," I explained, hoping for a "yes" reply.

"Friend, are you sure that this is what you want to do?"

"Yeah. Roz is bringing me the money in the morning," I replied.

By this time, my car was broken down, so Gina had to come get us from our house.

Pulling up to Gina's apartment complex parking lot, Haylen got out excited because she hadn't been to Gina's place in a while. Gina handed Haylen her keys so she could open the door to get in. Meanwhile, Gina wanted to talk.

Chapter Thirty-One

"Meagan, have the baby, and I'll help you out as much as I can," Gina said while firing up her Black & Mild cigar.

"Gina, my life is already going downhill. David is not watching Alex so I can work. Shit. If I do work full-time, then I'll just be paying for my bills and daycare," I said, rubbing my belly.

"Well, friend, whatever you want to do, I'll stand by you," she said, and we both started walking towards her apartment door.

Ring. Ring. Ring. Gina and I looked at another, then I said, "It's David calling."

"Answer, bitch!" she said, nudging me.

"Hello," I answered.

"Where you at?" David asked.

"I'm over Gina's house."

"Okay. I'm on my way."

"Noooo we 'bout to-," I could only say, then heard a *click*.

Gina was still looking at me. I said, "Bitch, he's on his way!" while putting the phone in the diaper bag.

Not even 10 minutes later, David was pulling into Gina's apartment complex parking lot. I walked over to his car, and he was firing up his Marlboro Red cigarette and exiting his car.

"Where's Alex?" David asked while trying to hug me.

I backed away from him and answered, "Upstairs in the house."

"So what are you going to do?" David asked.

"About what?" I replied.

"About the abortion - what's up?"

"Aw, well, Roz will be bringing me the money to pay for it in the morning," I answered.

His face had a glow, and with a smile. "Okay. That's good news!"

I instantly got sad and no longer wanted him in my presence.

"Yeah, this is what we have to do."

His phone kept ringing, and he just ignored each call without looking at his phone.

Meagan, why must you put up with such a man like this? I thought to myself.

David and I talked for a while, then he wanted to see Alex before he left, but Gina had already put Alex to bed for me.

"Well, let me know how everything went," David said while getting into his car.

"Yeah, I will," I said in a low voice, then watched him pull out of Gina's parking lot.

Deep down inside I knew he was on his way to be a dog while I'm trapped pregnant, about to kill our baby tomorrow.

As I entered Gina's apartment, she was sitting on the couch waiting for me.

"Where's Haylen?" I asked.

"Oh, she's in the room sleeping with Alex," she replied.

"So, Meagan, are you sure that this is what you want to do?" Gina asked.

"Yes," I lied.

"Okay," she replied.

Then I received a text message on my phone.

"It's David," I said to Gina.

"What he say?" Gina asked.

"I love you," I replied.

Gina just laughed. Then, when she noticed I wasn't laughing, she stopped.

"What's wrong, Meagan? You know he won't leave you alone," she said.

"I hate him!" I replied, and Gina's jaw dropped from my response.

Chapter Thirty-Two

My alarm clock from my phone was going off at 7 A.M., and I instantly jumped up.

"Let me call Roz," I said to myself, as I was reaching for my phone.

Ring. Ring. Ring. Ring. Ring. Ring.

"Shit. C'mon, Roz. Answer!" I said.

I hung the phone up and called back again. *Ring. Ring. Ring.*

"Hello," Roz answered, still sounding half asleep.

"Roz, you gonna bring me the money?" I asked.

"Yeah, where you at?" he asked with his voice all groggy.

I knew he had pulled an all-nighter making money so that he could give me the money for the abortion.

"I'm over Gina's house. She has to drop me off and pick me up from the abortion clinic," I explained.

"Okay. I'm about to come now," he said, then hung up.

Deep down in my heart, I knew what I was about to do was wrong, but I had to do this and take care of my kids and leave David the hell alone.

I placed the phone on the couch. Since my brother lived across town, I jumped in the shower with my mind flooding with thoughts of regrets before having the abortion.

You will regret this! You're a strong woman. Everything happens for a reason, Meagan, don't play God! I thought to myself.

As I got out of the shower, I was drying off, when I heard my brother's ringtone playing on my phone, so I knew he was either close or outside. I rushed, putting my clothes on so I could get to my phone and it stopped ringing. His Gucci Mane ringtone started playing again, and I jotted out of the bathroom to answer my phone.

"Hello," I answered.

"I'm outside," Roz said.

"Okay. I'm coming down now," I replied while rushing out the door.

There he was in his 2003 silver Lexus. I walked up to the driver side, and he rolled down the window and said, "Here's $600."

"Aw, thank you, Roz. You know I got you back, right?" I said, reaching for the money.

"Yep, call me, and let me know you're alright," he said while switching his gear switch into drive.

"I will, bruh love," I replied, and I watched as he drove off.

Walking back to Gina's apartment while looking up to the sky, I said, "Lord, forgive me for my sin that I'm about to commit."

Chapter Thirty-Three

"So, Ms. Guy, you're on your way to have the abortion procedure done. How were you feeling?" Dr. Martin asked with his eyes focused on me.

"I was sad, don't get me wrong, I didn't really want to do it. I guess the only reason why I wanted to have this abortion was because David was making a fool out of me, and I was so embarrassed. I felt humiliated. Here he was not even watching Alex. I can't work. I'm barely making ends meet, so I knew this was what I had to do," I replied with tears in my eyes.

Dr. Martin looked sad and continued to listen to me.

After I awakened Gina and got Haylen and Alex ready, we got into Gina's car and headed to the abortion clinic, which was just a few minutes away from where Gina stayed.

"Gina, now the lady who answered the phone at the abortion clinic said there may be protestors out, so you just got to keep driving," I explained.

"Okay. So what if they are on their property trying to stop you?" Gina asked.

"Naw. She also said that they aren't allowed on their property and that the police would be parked by their building, I guess to make sure everything will be okay," I explained.

Alex and poor Haylen were too young to know what was going on in the back seat of Gina's car. I was glad because later in life it would kill me to have to explain to them why I killed their little brother or sister.

At this time we were turning off Nicholasville Road onto Illinois Street where the abortion clinic was only to see a crowd of protestors. As we got closer, we could see adults and children holding up all different kinds of poster pictures of aborted babies. One poster read "Death Sold Here," and another read "The Killing Place."

I glanced to my left and saw a white man holding a protest poster reading "I'm a Child, Not a Choice," and to my right I saw a white woman holding up a protest poster reading "Thou Shall Not Kill." Adults were out there with little babies in their arms, and all I could do was make myself strong by ignoring these people. As Gina got closer to the protestors to pass them, some had jumped in front of her car with their arms out, motioning for her to stop.

Gina was slowing down and we could hear them shouting not to go any further.

"Gina, what are you doing? Keep going, keep going!" I yelled, and she put her foot on the gas, and the protestors jumped out of Gina's way, scared that she might hit one of them.

"Why did you try stopping? I told you that you weren't supposed to stop, Gina!" I said, still yelling.

"Damn, Meagan. What did you want me to do? Run them the fuck over?" Gina yelled back.

We were now entering into the abortion clinic's parking lot. And just like the lady had said, there was a policeman sitting in his car, parked on the main road in front of the abortion clinic, facing the protestors.

With my heart pounding fast, I got out of the car and fired up a cigarette to calm my nerves.

"Let me just smoke this, and we can go in so you can sign me in. You got your license on you, right?" I asked.

"Yeah," Gina said while getting out of the car.

I looked at the protestors across the street, and they were now watching me and chanting words that I couldn't really make out because there was some small distance between us.

I turned my attention away from them and looked at the abortion clinic's door, and I was literally five steps away, thinking, *Here I go off to kill my unborn child.*

"Friend, you sure you want to do this?" Gina asked, looking really sad.

I mean, by the look on her face was saying, "Pl*ease don't do it*," and that's when I heard a man's voice speaking through a megaphone saying, "Walk this way!"

I instantly turned, still with my cigarette in my hand, and all the protestors were looking at me. They then knew he caught my attention.

"God's not going to put too much on you that you can't bear. He loves you too much. That's why He says He'll never leave you nor forsake you," the man was speaking.

I glanced back at the abortion clinic door while the man was still speaking, and I could hear him clearly. That's when a black two-door car parked beside me. A couple who looked like they were in their early to late twenties jumped out of their car and walked straight into the abortion clinic with no hesitation, although they were also hearing this man through this megaphone preaching.

Instantly in my mind I assumed the man was making her have an abortion, and that she didn't want one. I only thought that because it was my situation. I mean, if the man wanted her to truly have the baby, why wouldn't she? If David didn't mention abortion, I sure wouldn't have been at the clinic.

Dr. Martin was just looking and said, "So it seems like you felt sorry for that lady?"

"Yeah, because they just walked into the building with no problem, I didn't know their situation nor do I really know if he was her man. He could have been one of her family members."

As I'm listening to the man telling me over and over to come to them, I glanced over to the cop who was sitting in his car. I could see that his windows were down, and I could tell he was wondering what I was going to do.

"Gina, I can't do this," I said, and I broke down crying.

She hugged me, and the man speaking into the megaphone kept repeating, "Jesus loves you!"

"Let's go, Meagan," Gina said while getting back into the car.

"Okay," I replied.

The protestors were cheering for joy. Gina then started up her car, and as we drove to pass the protestors, a lady jumped in front of the car motioning for us to stop. Gina looked at me for me to tell her what to do.

"You can stop," I said, and as soon as she did, the protestors reached with their arms out for hugs while praising God and Jesus.

As I stepped out of the car, the lady who stood out in front of the car said, "God bless you! God bless you!"

"My name is Jennifer, and that is my husband," she said, pointing to the gentleman who was speaking into the megaphone.

By this time he was making his way to me.

"Hello. I'm Collin, and I'm glad that you followed the Lord's words," he said.

His wife then went into detail, while rubbing her belly, how they had four children and were now expecting a set of twins.

"Can we say a prayer before you go?" she asked.

"Yes," I replied, and we all bowed our heads.

After saying our goodbyes and getting back into the car, Jennifer followed me and asked for my name.

"Meagan… Meagan Guy," I answered.

"We go to the United Church of God, and we will be praying for you," she said, and we drove off after I thanked her.

"Meagan, can I tell you something?" Gina asked.

"Yeah," I replied.

"I prayed last night for the Lord to give you a change of heart," Gina said with a smile.

All I could think about was how many people did that police officer witness having a change of heart just by the protestors speaking God's words.

Chapter Thirty-Four

Dr. Martin was smiling while nodding, and I could tell he enjoyed the happy ending.

"Okay. So after that experience how did you break the news to David?" Dr. Martin asked.

"Oh yeah - breaking the news to David. Well, a mutual friend of David and I had called me and told me how he was at work, and David and Dirty Di had come to place their fast food order. He mentioned that David had stepped outside for a moment, and that's when Dirty Di had told him how David was saying my son Alex wasn't his son."

"Okay. Let me get this straight. David wants you to have an abortion, and your brother had to pay for the abortion. Yet, while you're about to have an abortion, he's out with another woman… the nerve of him," Dr. Martin said.

I could tell that Dr. Martin was angry at David's evil doggish ways.

"Correct," I replied.

"You confronted him, right?" Dr. Martin asked.

"Hell yeah!" I snapped. "I called him and told him how I was told about him and Dirty Di being out together and how she was saying he was denying Alex to her. David didn't deny them being out together but he claimed that he didn't know that she said that. He also denied him denying Alex to her."

"So, did you believe him?" Dr. Martin asked.

"Hell no!" I replied. "First of all, he shouldn't have been out with any woman. Secondly, why does she have my son in her damn mouth? And last but not least, if he was claiming my child, I think my child would be to his house, and it wouldn't seem like he's sneaking around just to see our son," I explained.

Dr. Martin stood up from his chair and walked over to me on the loveseat.

"Ms. Guy, I hate that you had to go through all of this alone," he said.

"I was a total mess and knew that I had to do what I had to do, and that was to leave him alone and raise these kids," I replied.

I found a new hospital to deliver my baby. Months had passed, and I was finding myself going to the doctor's appointments by myself again. I was falling into deep depression, and nobody really knew. I was not happy to be carrying around my baby because I felt that everyone was laughing at me behind my back.

I knew what I had to do, so I signed up for college classes and went to the Cabinet for Family and Children's Office and signed up for welfare. By doing this, I was going to be approved for free childcare, which would help me out with Alex and this baby soon to come.

In August 2013, I signed up for four college classes, and boy was it a struggle dealing with pregnancy brain. I studied at home, which was hard because while helping Haylen with school work, cooking, cleaning, and taking care of an eight-month-old baby. Plus, being pregnant was very stressful and tiresome at times. A lot of my homework I had to do on the computer, and I didn't have a computer or internet. So Roz, who lived just a few minutes away, would come get me and the kids. He would take us with him to him and his girlfriend's house, just so I could use their computer and internet. They would cook and watch Haylen and Alex while I did my work.

"You got it all done?" Roz asked, as I closed up their Dell laptop computer.

"Yeah, I'm done. Thank you," I answered.

It would be dark outside when I got finished with the homework assignments at times. The saddest and embarrassing thing about this situation was that going to or leaving my brother's house we would pass David's street.

I felt bad that my little brother had to pick up and play a big brother role. I mean, he was only 21 years old with his own child to worry about, but instead he stuck by my side. I sometimes wonder how he truly felt knowing that he gave me the money to abort my baby and I didn't, after me knowing how David was with Alex.

"Pappy, just think, you'll be a radiologist if you just keep up the good work with school," Roz said.

I knew he was proud that I was going to school. I think that's why he stayed on me, constantly asking if I wanted to come to his house to do homework. There were even times he would have his clients come pick us up and drop us off when he totaled his Lexus, and I am and will always be so grateful to him. I think that's what pushed me to work harder, knowing I at least had my brother who believed in me.

Chapter Thirty-Five

I was happy when I found out I was having another son because Alex's clothes could be used again, and there wasn't too much stuff I would have to buy. I was still going to my doctor's appointments by myself, and David still wasn't inviting us to his house.

"He probably has a girl living with him," my mother said while helping me with Alex while I was washing dishes. "If David hasn't come to get Alex, he has a woman living with him!" she repeated, now rocking Alex back and forth.

I didn't respond because I felt it deep down inside, and I had had a dream that Dirty Di was at David's house and I got into a fight with her. That's when I heard my brother's ringtone on my phone.

"Hello," I answered.

"Pappy, dis nigga David is over here by the house with some girl," Roz said.

"What?!" I said while rushing outside so our mother couldn't hear our conversation.

"Yeah, I'm outside smoking a cigarette and dis nigga pulled up with some girl in the parking lot."

At this time I could hear Roz walking as he's explaining to me what was going on. Then I heard Roz say, "What's up, David?"

I hung the phone up, and my heart started beating fast. "Oh my gosh. Roz is talking to him," I whispered to myself.

As I walked back into the house, my mother asked, "What's going on?"

"Oh nothing," I lied, but I know my face told her I was lying.

She didn't say anything else, and I know she knew something was wrong. Roz's ringtone was playing again, and I didn't want to answer while our mother was still at the house. So I silenced the ringer and acted as if I was talking to someone.

"Hello. Oh no you have the wrong number. Oh, it's okay. Okay. Bye," I said. Then I pretended like I was hanging up, and I turned my phone off completely because I knew Roz was going to call right back.

My heart felt heavy and anxious to find out what was said, but I was also scared of what I was about to hear. Of all times my mother came to my house, I swear this was the longest that she stayed. I just need her to go so I can call Roz back and see what was going on.

"Well, Meagan, I guess I'll be leaving. It's getting dark, and I don't like driving at night," my mother said, as she was grabbing her belongings.

About time, I thought to myself.

As soon as my mother was getting into her car, I was dialing Roz's number.

Chapter Thirty-Six

"Pappy!" Roz answered.

"Yeah, what happened? Mama was over here, and I didn't want her to know anything," I explained.

"Dis nigga was picking up one of his twins 'cause one of them had to go to the hospital. So when I see him, dis nigga was spooked, explaining himself, so he went into the house, and ol' girl was still in the car. And she was telling me how David had a daughter with another woman, and I was like, 'Yeah, and he has a son, too!'"

I lost it. "Fuck that shit. This bitch needs to mind her own damn business!" I yelled, then hung the phone up and instantly called David.

"Hello," David answered on the first ring.

I'm pretty sure he knew I was going to be calling since my brother had seen him and Dirty Di together.

"Why the fuck is that bitch still running her mouth, as if she doesn't know about my child, David?" I yelled through the phone. "Give me her number so I can tell her how the fuck I feel!"

David, acting dumb and confused as usual, was saying, "She knows Alex is my son. What's going on?"

I explained what Roz had told me, yet he refused to give me Dirty Di's number.

"That's okay, 'cause I'm on my way to your house!" I screamed, and hung up the phone.

David knew my car was down, and I've never been to his house since the day he showed us. What he didn't know was that I had reached my fuck it point. I'm tired of this bitch and his old doggish ass, so I called up Roz again.

"Yeah, Pappy," Roz answered.

"Bruh, you got a car?" I asked.

"Yeah, I got one of my people's cars. What's up?" he asked.

"Come get me so I can go up to David's house," I said, still angry as hell.

"Yep, I'll be there in a minute. I'm 'bout to leave out now," Roz said.

I put on some girl boxer shorts with a too-little light blue wife beater that was showing off half of my belly, I was looking like Winnie the Pooh. I then grabbed a pair of my black and green K-Swiss tennis shoes and tied them as tightly as I could. I called my cousin Latoya on the phone to let her know she might be watching my kids while I'm in jail, and Roz was going to have to come bond me out.

"What's going on, Meagan?" Latoya asked, but before I could explain, Roz was outside blowing the car horn.

"Girl, I'll call you back. Roz is here," I said, then hung up the phone.

I grabbed Alex and put him in his baby car seat and called for Haylen to come out of her room. I opened the door, and Roz got out of the red SUV to help carry and put Alex in the car. Haylen followed, and I locked the house up and got into the car.

We all buckled up our seatbelts, and Roz looked at me, then said, "Well, since you know exactly where he lives, why don't you drive?"

So Roz and I got out to exchange seats. I put the car in reverse and started backing out of my driveway, and all I could think was, *Here it goes.*

As we pulled up in David's driveway, we noticed the lights were on throughout his house. As I was gripping the car's steering wheel, I could feel my palms were sweaty.

"Y'all wait here," I said, as I opened the driver's side door to get out.

With each step getting closer to David's door, I got a funny feeling in my stomach telling me to turn around and get back in the car and go home. As badly as I wanted and needed to, with my adrenaline so pumped up, my body wouldn't let me turn around. Because with all this anger and hurt that I've been feeling, I needed answers, and I wasn't planning on waiting another day.

I opened his screen door and then turned the doorknob. It was locked, so I rang the doorbell continuously and started banging on the door at the same time, and that's when David's door slowly opened.

Chapter Thirty-Seven

"Yes, Meagan," David said with the door slightly opened.

"Let's call the bitch now!" I demanded while holding the screen door open.

David didn't seem like he was going to invite me in, and by the look on his face, it looked like he was trying to hide something.

"She's here?" I asked.

Next thing I know, I barged into David's house, looking into the kitchen, but there was no sign of Dirty Di. I walked into the two bedrooms and bathroom, yet there was no sign of her. And I saw that David's bedroom door was closed. I reached for the handle and turned it. It was locked, and then I started banging and kicking on the door.

"Come on out, bitch! Come out so you can see my son - OUR son since you always have something to say about him!" I screamed through the door.

"Girl, I ain't even in the mood," Dirty Di replied through the door.

I could see David out of the peripheral of my eye, and he looked scared. He just watched from the hallway as I tried to break down his bedroom door to get to her.

"Bitch, I'm gonna fuck you up! Open this door, bitch!" I yelled, still trying to beat down the door.

I then turned away from the door and walked into the living room, opened the screen door, and motioned for Roz and the kids to come inside. By this time, David was nervous because he didn't know Roz was in the car.

Roz stepped out of the car, and I told him to bring Alex and Haylen into the house, and I stormed my ass back to David's bedroom door.

"Bitch, come out of the room! My son is here! Come out, and see what he looks like!" I yelled.

There was no response, and I figured she was probably at this time calling someone on her phone to come jump me. I then went back to the living room where now David was sitting on the couch with pure shame covered all over his face. Not only my brother has to witness his deadbeat, trifling, double-life living ass, but also my daughter, Haylen. Poor Alex not knowing what was going on, I think that's why I went up there. He was no longer going to be kept a secret.

As I looked at Alex just sitting in his baby car seat in the middle of the living room, I thought, *This is only his second time in this house.* And anger took over me, and I see the 55-inch flat screen television and thought to myself, *Push that motherfucker over*, and that's exactly what I did.

"Meagan!" Roz shouted, and I grabbed the baby's car seat, and Haylen's hand, following behind Roz.

Holding back tears until I get in the car, David came outside and stood on the porch. We were getting the kids in the car, and right when I opened the driver's side door to get in, David shouted, "Are you done?!"

I shut the car door, turned around, and while walking towards him I yelled, "Hell naw, I ain't done! You got this bitch in this house!" and I gave him a smooth clean two piece.

It happened so fast that even Roz got out of the car to stop me from hitting David, but it was too late. David staggered towards the bushes next to his porch.

"Yeah, dog, you had that one coming," Roz said while looking at David who was trying to regain his balance.

"I'm calling the police!" David said, and Roz, the kids, and I backed out of David's driveway.

"I can't believe him!" I cried out while beating on the steering wheel.

Everyone in the car was silent, listening to me cry out my hurt.

"Pappy, the police are behind us," Roz said, in a calm voice.

I looked through the rearview mirror while drying my face with my hands, and surely there was a white police car behind us.

"Fuck!" I yelled.

Chapter Thirty-Eight

I stopped at the stop sign, turned on my left blinker, turned left, and so did the police. I then reached a red light and turned my left blinker on again. The light turned green, and I turned left, and so did the police car. By this time I was nervous. And although I knew everyone had on their seatbelts, I still asked, "Does everyone have on their seatbelts?" He's going to pull us over any minute, so I made sure I drove the exact speed limit, which was thirty-five.

Since David and I lived 3-5 minutes away, depending on the lights, I was almost home, and the police car was still following us. I reached the last light where I would have to take another left turn to get to my street, so I turned my left blinker on once again and turned, only for the police car to continue going straight.

I let out a loud sigh. I was so thankful that I wasn't going to jail at this moment, but my heart was broken because I just saw for myself that David was happy with his lifestyle. I came to accept that he picked a woman over our son.

Two weeks passed without me talking to David. I must admit I was hurt, but by me going to school and having homework and exams kept me busy from constantly thinking about what had happened at David's house. I was sitting on my bed writing a speech for my public speaking class when my phone rang. I glanced over and saw it was David calling.

"What the hell does he want?" I asked myself.

I just let it ring and continued writing my speech. The phone started ringing again, and once again it was David, and once again I let the phone ring. I wonder why he's calling, like what the hell does he have to say?

It wasn't until the third time David called when I just cut my phone off completely. I was actually proud of myself. I have my children and school to worry about, not David. He's no longer relevant in my life.

As I finished my speech, I stood up and was practicing in my bedroom mirror when I heard a knock at my front door. I walked down my stairs as the knock was getting louder and louder, then I heard my screen door close. I swung my door open, and to my surprise, it was David and his twins.

Chapter Thirty-Nine

"What do you want, David?" I asked through the screen door.

"Meagan, I'm sorry," David said.

"Okay, but what are you doing at my house?" I asked.

David then looked down at his twins, I guess to tell me that he didn't want to discuss anything in front of them.

"Well, I have a speech to practice for tomorrow, so I'll talk to you later," I said, and started to close my door.

"Meagan, I need you!" David yelled.

I closed the door and locked it, then leaned my back against the door. I heard the screen door open, and David said, "Meagan, she's gone. Please open the door!"

I was so hurt. I shouted through the door, "Leave me alone, and go away!"

I walked away from the door, headed for the stairs, and I heard the screen door shut. I turned around and walked to the living room window only to see David and his twins sitting on my porch.

Meagan, go to your room and finish your essay, a voice in my head said.

David was looking like a sad lost puppy, and I didn't care at all. I turned and walked up the stairs to my room and shut the door and continued to practice for my public speaking speech.

Chapter Forty

Days turned into weeks then weeks into months, and David was stepping up to the plate. He was spending more time with Alex and inviting us to his house. David even was cooking for us and trying to be a family man. Deep down inside, I felt sad and lonely still because David has shown me that I was his second option. I was still going to the doctor by myself, but he was watching Alex while I studied, and that's all I had wanted from him, to be a father to our son.

It was getting closer and closer to my due date as the fall semester was ending.

"Hello, David, I'm at the hospital. Roz and his girlfriend is here with me. Where you at?" I asked.

"Oh, my uncle has passed away. I'm on my way to Baltimore," David replied.

My heart dropped. "Oh okay," I said, trying to gather myself so that David wouldn't hear the disappointment, and so Roz wouldn't see my hurt.

"Well, I've dilated to 3 centimeters, and they're keeping me. It's Thursday, so when will you be back?"

"I'll be back Monday," David replied.

"I guess I'll send you pictures because I should have this baby today or tomorrow," I said.

"Okay. That will be nice," David said.

"Well, I'm about to get off the phone so I can get some rest," I lied.

"Okay… Meagan," David said.

"Yes," I replied.

"You know I wish I was there?" David asked.

"Yeah, I hear you," I replied, then hung up the phone.

December, Friday the 13th, two days after Alex's first birthday, that's when Kevin, my handsome son was born - all 7 pounds and 19 ½ inches of him.

Chapter Forty-One

David and I were growing closer and closer. Living in two separate house-holds was stressful at times, since the money that we could have been saving if we were living together, we were spending on bills.

"Meagan, let's move together under one roof?" David suggested.

"Hahahahaha! You must be crazy," I replied.

I was folding clothes to put into my dresser drawers.

"Let's get married, and you get off of welfare and Section 8, and we'll get a house together, and you can get a car, and you just stay at home and just finish school," David went on.

"David, look. We are not going to move together, and besides, I would have never been on welfare if you would have just watched Alex so I could work. But noooooooo, you moved that bitch, along with her grown ass kids in with you. So hell to the naw we ain't moving together!" I replied.

David, who was pairing up socks, looked at me and said, "I love you, and I can't see you being with no one else!"

I must admit that David and I were having sex from time to time, but deep down, I knew he was still messing around with other women. As much as I loved him, I put up a front as if I didn't care just because he had already hurt me so badly.

Alex, Kevin, and Haylen were watching Disney Channel, and David's twins were with David's good friend, Lucy. She was a nice lady. The only problem I had with her was that they were calling her, "Mama," which I didn't like, and put a stop to.

"Well, I need to get my work uniform from home - that's if I can spend the night," David said.

I glanced over at him and rolled my eyes.

"You don't want me to?" David asked.

"It's whatever you want to do, David."

"Okay, I'll be back," David said, then got up.

I heard his car start up, and just when I stood up from my bed to go downstairs to lock the front door, I felt sick to my stomach all of a sudden. I sat back down on my bed, holding my stomach with both hands and started gagging. I stood up and darted straight to the bathroom, raised the seat to the toilet and threw up.

Chapter Forty-Two

Days went by, and I was worried to death.

"I cannot be pregnant!" I said to myself.

I was pacing back and forth in my bedroom. I stopped when I reached the dresser and looked through my mirror.

"Who are you, Meagan?" I asked myself. "What are you doing? People are going to talk about you, and Mama, she's going to be upset."

I pulled out my dresser drawer and grabbed my pregnancy test that I had taken yesterday. I was really embarrassed, and I just knew that I was gonna be the talk of the family, friends, and nursing homes.

"I can't keep this child, God!" I yelled out aloud. "I can't do it, I'm not going to do it. No! Not this time," I yelled, and then my phone rung.

"Hello," I answered, trying to catch my breath.

"Meagan, what's up?" David asked.

"I'm fucking pregnant AGAIN, David!" I snapped.

There was a pure silence on both ends of the line for a few minutes until sounding like a broken record David said, "We can't afford it, Meagan. We have to get rid of it."

"I know, David. I already fucking know!" I yelled through the phone, and then hung up.

As I tossed my phone onto my bed, it started ringing again. I didn't even bother to look at it because I knew it was David calling. I was so not in the mood to keep hearing how we needed to have an abortion because I already fucking knew.

Here it is, I thought - I'm still in school, I'm on welfare with three kids that I'm struggling with already, and a car that's breaking down every few months. My bills were kicking my ass so I was constantly robbing Peter to pay Paul. But whenever I would look at my three beautiful children, they kept me focused and reminded me that they are the reason I'm going to school to make something of myself, so when they get older they could say, "I can do it because my mama did!"

I had applied for a school student loan, and the money had reached my account, and all I could do was think about the abortion. Night had fallen, and I got the kids to sleep and kneeled by my bed on my knees.

"Now I lay me down to sleep, I pray the Lord my soul to keep, if I shall die before I awake, I pray the Lord my soul to take. Lord, I dearly need you right now..."

Tears began falling down my face. "I need you to open up my eyes and my ears because tomorrow I'm calling the abortion clinic, and I'm doing this this time. I know you said you wouldn't put too much on me that I can't bear, but Lord, I'm telling you that I can't bear this child. I'm already talked about, and I'm living a stressful life, and you showed me over and over how David wasn't the right man for me. So I'm asking you to give me a sign to not abort this child. If you do give me a sign, then I won't abort. I need you, Heavenly Father, to show or tell me!" I yelled up to the ceiling. I then felt stupid because here I was taking my anger out on the Lord, so I raised up from off my knees and said, "Amen!" then got in the bed.

I must say I pray regularly, but I've never had prayer pouring out my heart. As loud as I was praying and crying, I was surprised I didn't wake up Alex and Kevin, who were sound asleep, still in my bed. I kissed them both and turned on my side and went straight to sleep.

Chapter Forty-Three

Morning came, and I was awakened by my alarm clock on my phone. As I reached for my phone to turn off the alarm, the time read 7:00 A.M.. I looked over at Alex and Kevin, who were still peacefully spread out, sleeping in my bed. I said to myself aloud, "Call the abortion clinic."

As I googled the abortion clinic's name, their number popped up, so I pressed dial. *Ring. Ring. Ring. Ring. Ring. Ring.* Then the answering machine came on telling me their hours of operation, which were 8 A.M. until 4 P.M., and that I could leave a message and someone would get back with me. I hung up the phone, I was an hour early calling, so I could get me and the kids ready for work, school and daycare, and then have Alice to work before 9:00 A.M.. Haylen's school bus picked her up for school. So Alice, the boys, and I got into my car.

We were dropping Alice off to her restaurant job that she hated at times, and even though 8:00 A.M. passed, the abortion was on my mind. As soon as I got to my job, I was going to call the abortion clinic back.

Alice got out of the car, blowing the boys kisses, and said, "Meagan, I get off at 5 P.M.."

"I'll be here to get you, ma'am," I responded.

Since she had some time before her shift started, she pulled her cigarette and lighter out of her black jacket and fired up her cigarette. I waved goodbye then pulled off.

As I headed to the boys' daycare, all I could think about was getting this abortion over with. I knew for a fact I was not going to get pregnant again after this abortion by David! I must admit I didn't feel bad about doing this this time because I was too embarrassed and ashamed.

I was always tired, barely had energy to take care of my kids. Plus, I still had people in my business wondering how many kids I had and by whom. You know, it's sad when you don't want anyone knowing who your kids' father is because you don't want to hear anything about who he's messing around with. I reached the boys' daycare and signed them both in and carried them to their classroom. Giving hugs and kisses, I headed out the building, and now, I was rushing to my job.

As I was pulling into the parking lot at the Help Center, Mrs. Jackson was waving and smiling at me while walking up the wooden ramp to un-lock the back door of the building. I worked 20 hours a week at the Help Center through a Federal Work-Study Program while attending school, while I was receiving welfare.

I parked and rushed out of the car because she had left the back door open, and Lord knows, it's already cold in there, and we don't need more cold air entering the building.

I walked up the wooden ramp, and then into the building, and sure enough, it was cold. I could hear Mrs. Jackson in the kitchen warming up something in the microwave, which actually smelled good.

"Good morning, Mrs. Jackson," I called out, as I walked through the computer room and headed to the front of the building.

My everyday routine was to put out the jobs available sign in the front yard, cutting on all the computers in the computer room, entering usernames and passwords, and waiting on the public to come in to ask for our services. Mrs. Jackson walked into the front, where I was now sitting at the desk.

"Good morning, Ms. Guy," she said while holding a cup of hot choco-late in a white coffee mug. She then took a sip and asked, "So have you figured out what you're going to do with this baby?"

"Yeah, I'm going to abort it. I called this morning, and they were closed so I have to call them back."

Then the other ladies who worked there at the center through the school were showing up, which cut our conversation short. As we started getting busy, with people coming in for our services, I was thinking, *After I'm through with this person, I'm gonna call the abortion clinic back.*

That morning was busy at the Help Center with us sending out people to have interviews, helping make resumes, calling in God's Pantry referrals, and at noon, it finally slowed down. With four more hours left until quitting time, Mrs. Jackson shocked all of us and told us we could have the rest of the day off and still have our time.

We all were surprised and happy because Mrs. Jackson rarely let us leave early. The first thing I thought was, *Let me go home and take a nap, and then I'll call the abortion clinic.* I got into my car exhausted and tired and drove home. As I pulled up to my house, my body knew it was about to rest.

As I got into the house, I climbed up the stairs, kicked off my shoes, and laid across my bed.

Just an hour nap, I planned, and then I'd call to schedule my appointment at the abortion clinic. I closed my eyes with no regret of what I was about to do, and then my phone rung.

"Fuuuuuckkkk!" I screamed, as I searched for my phone in the bed. "Yeah, Alice," I answered with an attitude.

"Meagan, they let me off early," Alice replied.

I took a deep breath, "Okay, I'm on my way!" I said, then hung the phone up.

I put my shoes back on, went down the stairs, and all I could think was how tired I was, and I got in my car and headed to McDonald's. While I was at the red light waiting to turn left to be at McDonald's, there was some kind of construction going on in the middle of the road.

I remember it like it was yesterday. It was cold outside, and it was a standstill at this red light. I know the light had changed to green about three to four times. I then took my attention from the light and the construction workers and looked at the bumper of the car in front of me. My heart dropped, as I read the bumper sticker, which read "Abortion is murder, no matter how they are sliced," in red.

"Abortion is murder, no matter how they are sliced," I reread again. I quickly grabbed my phone and started taking pictures. It's like right after that, the construction workers finished with whatever they were doing, and we then were allowed to move. And as the car in front of me started moving, I then noticed the car's license plate read, "JS-LORD."

To be continued…